BREAKING BREAD

FATHER DOMINIC GARRAMONE, OSB

First Edition, Fourth Printing

ISBN 0-9674652-2-2

Printed in the United States of America by Inland Press/Inland Book, Menomonee Falls, Wisconsin.

KETC
3655 Olive St.
St. Louis, MO 63108

Visit the *Breaking Bread With Father Dominic* Web site at *http://www.breaking-bread.com.* Instructional videotapes from the *Breaking Bread With Father Dominic* television program may be ordered at 1-800-293-5949.

*Breaking Bread With Father Dominic* is underwritten by Fleischmann's Yeast.

# TABLE OF CONTENTS

# Table of Contents

# TABLE OF CONTENTS

*Editor:*
Terri Gates

*Art directors:*
Jennifer Snyder
Emily Mitchell

*Recipe editor:*
Barbara Gibbs Ostmann

*Illustrator:*
Michael Neville

*Cover photo:*
Gregg Goldman

# About the Author

In his 40 years, Father Dominic Garramone has managed to achieve a number of his life goals. Four milestones top his list. Academically, he earned a bachelor's and two Master's degrees, all summa cum laude. He joined St. Bede Abbey and became the head of its drama department. And in 1992, he was ordained to the priesthood.

He chose another goal while lunching with his grandmother in a Denver café. Nearby he overheard employees of an advertising firm discuss ideas for a campaign. Enchanted by their creative banter, Father Dom added to his list the goal of being part of a professional creative team. And he wanted to be on television.

Remarkably, he realized those objectives through his public television program, *Breaking Bread With Father Dominic.* Although he envisioned his broadcast debut as a standup comic on *The Tonight Show,* he happily recognizes that *Breaking Bread With Father Dominic* has helped him achieve yet more goals: to write a book (he's now the author of three), to give his students the opportunity to experience a professional television environment, and to be in Busch Stadium to see Mark McGwire hit a home run (luckily, his TV show is taped in St. Louis, where the slugger plays for the Cardinals).

What's left on Father Dom's list? Well, after he designs and builds a new school auditorium for St. Bede, he'd like to write a book on domestic spirituality; arrange an ongoing school program to give more students the chance to experience TV production first-hand; sit with his family and friends in the Busch Stadium section behind home plate "where you get free food"; and sample bread while visiting Potenza, Italy, where his ancestors lived.

Father Dom even has a few more baking goals. First, he'd like his food-stylist friend to teach him how to make paper-thin strudel. Then, he wants to make pecan rolls as good as his Grandma Gome's. Third, he wants to learn to make bread in a Dutch oven over the embers of a campfire. And finally, like bakers everywhere, he wants to make the perfect pie crust.

# Introduction

## HOW I DEVELOP RECIPES

People often ask me how I come up with bread recipes, or where I get ideas for variations on classic breads. There isn't any one answer to the question, really. Some recipes develop spontaneously by what's in the fridge in the abbey kitchen (like the Blue Cheese Walnut Bread, page 81) or what's leftover from last night's supper (like the mashed potatoes in Hungarian Potato Bread, page 113). Some are given to me by friends (Danish Pastry Dough, page 69) or people I've come into contact with because of the program (the authentic Parker House Rolls recipe, page 26, is the best example). If you bake regularly and often speak with other Bread Heads (my sister's term for fans of the show), it's not hard to collect recipes.

But for the most part, my recipes are based on careful research paired with reckless experimentation. Let's suppose I want to develop a recipe for a classic bread like Anadama (page 32). I'll begin by finding as many different recipes for anadama bread as I can, researching in cookbooks, magazines and on the Internet. Then I'll make a chart with which I can easily compare the ingredients and their proportions and add notes at the bottom about method.

Once my chart is made, I look to see if there are constants, which indicate a necessary ingredient. In the case of anadama bread, cornmeal and molasses are ingredients sine qua non. I check the proportion of yeast to flour (about one package yeast per 3 or 4 cups flour is the norm) and if the recipe has strong flavors or a lot of sugar, I'll consider using fast-rising yeast instead of the usual active dry yeast. Remember that for active dry yeast, lukewarm liquids (100 to 110 degrees) are used whereas for fast-rising yeast, the liquids are heated to 120 to 130 degrees; check each recipe carefully.

I might also decide that the yield of the recipe needs to be reduced or increased. Does the recipe make too much bread for an average family, or is the bread good enough that you'll want plenty? Then I look to see if I can make the recipe more healthful by reducing the amount of fat or salt, maybe by changing flours or flavorings. Sometimes the recipe gets changed just because I don't like a particular flavor (cilantro, caraway and black walnuts rarely make their way into my baking!). If the recipe calls for eggs, I always use Grade A large, fresh from a local egg farm.

By now I have a pretty good sense of the recipe and probably have one or two variations on paper or in my head. Then it's time to go to the kitchen and start mixing. I keep careful records of amounts, sometimes making two different versions at the same time. I might try kneading the same dough for 6, 8, 10 and 12 minutes, just to see what it does to the quality of the dough (6 minutes is more than enough for Chocolate Chunk Bread, page 46, while 12 minutes of kneading is ideal for Nine-Grain Bread, page 20). Whatever the time spent, kneading continues to be one of the most enjoyable aspects of baking. The rhythm of "pull back, roll forward, quarter turn" lends itself to relaxing the mental muscles and meditating.

I also play with shaping the bread—braided or free form?—or perhaps try an unusual pan. Some recipes require special pans although I'm not afraid to break the rules on that either. When a recipe calls for a baking sheet, I recommend using the thickest metal jelly-roll pan you can find. There are baking sheets and cookie pans that have double bottoms with an air pocket in between; the pan's design helps keep the bottom of the bread from darkening too quickly, but using them may also increase your baking time. When using loaf pans, be sure to use the size specified in each recipe—I tried these breads in various pans and have listed the sizes that give the best results.

Baking temperatures and times are crucial as well and need to be well documented during the experimentation phase. Breads are generally baked at temperatures ranging from 350 degrees to 425 degrees. Breads with more sugar (Hero Sandwich Bread, page 34) are best baked at a lower temperature, while a simple bread like French Baguettes (page 107) can be baked at 400 degrees or higher. I also test baking times by using an instant-read thermometer to measure the interior temperature of the bread. Fully baked bread will have an interior temperature between 190 degrees and 205 degrees. Soft rolls and batter bread will tend toward the lower end, while heavy multigrain breads should be baked above 200 degrees.

After I have a recipe I like, I'll bake it exactly the same way two or three more times, just to be sure I can get consistent results. These breads are, of course, tested on my fellow monks. I know I have a winner when Father Marion sidles up to me after breakfast and says, "I don't think you've got that recipe quite right. You'll need to test that on us at least four or five more times!" My interns David and Chris were very helpful during the testing process as well, taking samples home to their families and reporting their reactions. The finished recipe is then entered into my computer, I add the "Bread Break" notes, and then print out a copy for my three-ring binder in the abbey kitchen.

Once I'm satisfied with a recipe, I send it on to a professional food editor for review. Yeast recipes also go to the test kitchens at Fleischmann's Yeast. They test the recipes by conventional method, then develop a bread machine version. Sharp-eyed Bread Heads reading this cookbook will notice some occasional variation in the proportion of ingredients between the traditional recipe and the bread machine version. This is sometimes necessary in order to get consistent results in a variety of bread machines, although not every recipe can be converted to that format. Look for the symbol below for the bread machine version of a particular recipe.

I hope you will enjoy trying the recipes in this book, and that you'll eventually become confident enough to develop your own variations. It would please me very much if I inspire you to do a little reckless experimentation in your kitchen, such that you come up with a bread recipe uniquely your own that becomes a family favorite. You've heard me say it before: It's bread—it's going to forgive you!

"There are people in the world so hungry that God cannot appear to them except in the form of bread."

—Mahatma Gandhi (1869–1948)

# ALL GOOD GRAINS

When I first started baking, there were very few kinds of flour available. At the local Kroger in the next block you could find all-purpose white, some whole wheat, cake flour and a few sacks of rye flour on the bottom shelf. The bread aisle reflected the same limited selections: white bread, wheat bread, rye bread and pastries.

Today if you walk down the flour aisle of a large supermarket, you might discover a staggering variety of flours, including high-gluten flour milled specifically for bread baking, organic and stone-ground flours, and bread mixes for everything from nine-grain bread to focaccia to lemon poppy seed scones. If the store has a special nutrition or health food section, you might find amaranth, teff, quinoa and blue cornmeal, along with millet, flaxseed and multigrain mix in bulk.

I have seen a similar expansion in resources for Bread Heads. Entire catalogs of bowls, special tools, baking pans and serving baskets are now available. The development of bread machines has resulted in an explosion of bread cookbooks, and the Internet has made literally thousands of recipes accessible. We're in the middle of a bread renaissance, and it's exciting to have so many advantages readily available.

And yet none of these recent developments is of any use without the Bread Head's single most important kitchen utensil: an open mind. All the cookbooks in the Library of Congress won't help you if you're afraid to try new things. A number of the recipes in this chapter came about because I was challenged by something I'd never seen before. A viewer sent an e-mail suggesting that I explore blue cornmeal, and I combined it with a recipe my sister had sent me. I read about yeasted waffles in *The Fannie Farmer Cookbook* and wondered if I could make them lower in fat and higher in fiber. Mike the Deli Guy wanted to bake his own nine-grain bread instead of driving 70 miles to a bakery and asked me if I could develop a recipe. I've had some spectacular failures along the way, but that has made the final successes all the more satisfying.

I hope you enjoy the multigrain recipes in this chapter. More importantly, I hope you look at one of them and start wondering, "What would happen if I…?"

# Amaranth Blue Cornmeal Bread

Yield: 1 loaf.

½ cup **dried cherries**

⅓ cup boiling **water**

1 cup **all-purpose flour**

¼ cup **amaranth flour**
(see note)

1 cup **blue cornmeal**
(see note)

½ cup **granulated sugar**

½ teaspoon **salt**

1 ½ teaspoons **baking powder**

½ cup (1 stick) **butter**, melted

¼ cup **orange marmalade**, warmed

1 ¼ cups **milk**

2 **eggs**, beaten

⅓ cup **slivered almonds**

½ teaspoon **almond extract**

Put dried cherries in bowl and add boiling water; let stand 30 minutes to plump. Drain well before using.

Combine all-purpose flour, amaranth flour, cornmeal, sugar, salt and baking powder in a medium bowl; stir to mix. Combine melted butter, marmalade and milk in another bowl; stir to mix. Pour milk mixture into flour mixture. Add eggs; stir briefly. Gently fold in drained cherries, almonds and almond extract; batter will be lumpy. Do not overmix.

Pour batter into lightly greased 9x5x3 loaf pan. Bake in preheated 400-degree oven 35 to 45 minutes, or until lightly browned and a toothpick inserted in the center comes out clean. Let cool in pan on wire rack about 15 minutes, then remove from pan and let cool completely.

*Note: Amaranth is a tiny, seed-like grain that was grown in great quantities by the Aztecs. It is high in protein (one cup contains 28 grams) and has a unique, earthy flavor. You'll find amaranth flour at health food stores, or in the nutrition section of a large supermarket. Blue cornmeal is a product of the American Southwest. It adds an interesting color to this recipe. You can substitute white or yellow cornmeal if you can't find blue, but it's worth the effort to search, if only to expand your culinary education.*

## Bread Break

My sister Angela regularly sends me bread recipes from magazines and newspaper articles, often with notes about her own kitchen testing. This corn bread recipe was based on one that she had sent me, which I adapted and baked for the first time during the taping of our *Flour Power* episode in season three. Yes, I really did make the bread "live and without a net" without any previous testing. The orange marmalade I used on camera for this recipe was a whiskey marmalade that my field producer Anne-Marie brought back from Ireland just a couple of days before. I remembered it was in the fridge as the cameras were rolling! Much of my recipe development happens in just such a spontaneous fashion, and I encourage my viewers to do the same.

# SOURDOUGH CRACKED WHEAT BREAD WITH SUNFLOWER SEEDS

Yield: 2 loaves.

## Bread Break

I developed my sourdough
starter by the traditional
method (what did you
expect?) of placing a bowl of
batter on a warm window-
sill and waiting for it to
attract the wild yeast out of
the air. My batter was made
of filtered water, skim milk,
bread flour, whole wheat
flour and honey. I beat the
ingredients until smooth
with a wooden spoon, cov-
ered the bowl with nylon
net to keep the bugs out, and
put the bowl on the window-
sill of the kitchen on Holy
Saturday afternoon. By
Easter Monday, yeast was
bubbling happily in the
bowl. I let the yeast develop
for three days, then made
my first batch of sourdough
bread.

When you use a cup of
starter, you must replenish
the remaining starter with a
cup of flour and a scant cup
of water so the yeast can
continue to feed and multiply. Occasionally I'll add a
drop of honey or a table-

### STARTER (see Bread Break):

1 cup **filtered water**
(non-chlorinated)

1 cup **skim milk**

1 cup **bread flour**

1 cup **whole wheat flour**

1 teaspoon **honey**

1 package **FLEISCHMANN'S Active Dry Yeast**
(optional)

### SPONGE:

1 cup lukewarm **water**

2 tablespoons **dark corn syrup**

2 cups **bread flour**

1 cup **whole wheat flour**

### DOUGH:

1 package **FLEISCHMANN'S Active Dry Yeast**

1 cup lukewarm **water**

2 tablespoons **dark corn syrup**

2 teaspoons **salt**

¹/₄ teaspoon **baking soda**

¹/₂ cup **cracked wheat**

¹/₂ cup **unsalted sunflower seed kernels**, toasted

1 cup **whole wheat flour**

3 cups **bread flour**, divided

**For starter:** Combine water, milk, bread flour, whole wheat flour and honey in non-reactive bowl. Mix well with a wooden spoon. Cover bowl with open-weave cheesecloth and place outside on a warm, breezy day. The idea is to capture the wild yeast strains out of the air. Leave it out for several hours, or until the batter starts to develop bubbles and a pleasantly sour smell. Bring it inside and leave it in a warm place 2 or 3 days while the yeast develops. You might need to replenish the liquid each day; I often add more flour, as well. (There are no guarantees with this traditional method. If after three days the batter smells unpleasant or seems a bit slimy, throw it out, sterilize the bowl and try again.)

14

Or, make the starter with commercial yeast for a more reliable technique. Follow the directions, adding dry yeast along with the other ingredients. Leave in a warm place, covered with plastic wrap, for several days while the sour flavor develops. The starter will be sour, but not quite so wild tasting, and it will develop faster.

Once your starter is bubbling away, you can begin using it to make sourdough bread. You'll use 1 cup starter for most recipes. Replace that amount with equal amounts of flour and water. Place the replenished starter in a Mason jar or crock with a tight-fitting lid. Leave out for a couple of hours to develop, then close the lid and refrigerate for up to one week. The starter must be replenished once a week, so even if you don't use it to bake, take some out and feed the remainder with fresh liquid and flour.

**For sponge:** At least one day before baking, prepare sponge. Combine 1 cup sourdough starter, water, corn syrup, bread flour and whole wheat flour in a large non-metallic bowl; beat until mixture is smooth. Do not use metal utensils, only wooden or plastic. Cover bowl with plastic wrap. Let the sponge develop at room temperature for 24 to 72 hours. The longer you let the sponge develop, the stronger the distinctive sourdough flavor will be in your bread.

**For dough:** On the day of baking, stir down the sponge. In another bowl, dissolve yeast in lukewarm water. Stir in corn syrup, salt and baking soda; mix well. Add yeast mixture to sponge; beat until smooth. Stir in cracked wheat, sunflower kernels and whole wheat flour. Stir in 2 cups of the bread flour until thoroughly incorporated. Stir in remaining bread flour, about $1/4$ cup at a time, to make a cohesive dough.

Turn out dough onto a lightly floured surface. Knead 8 to 10 minutes, adding small amounts of flour as needed to keep dough manageable. Dough will be firm but still slightly sticky. Divide dough in half, and form each piece into a loaf. Place loaves in lightly greased $8 \frac{1}{2} \times 4 \frac{1}{2} \times 2 \frac{1}{2}$-inch loaf pans. Cover with a dry cloth and let rise in a warm, draft-free place about 45 minutes, or until nearly doubled.

About 15 minutes before end of rising time, preheat oven to 375

spoon of mashed potatoes to give the yeast an extra boost. Keep the starter in a crock or canning jar in the fridge until you're ready to use it. If you don't use it every week or so, pour some down the drain and replenish the starter with fresh water and flour.

degrees. Bake loaves 45 to 50 minutes, or until tops are lightly browned and bottom of loaf sounds hollow when tapped. Remove from pans and let cool on wire racks.

**Note:** *For this recipe, I streamlined the process by eliminating a first rising for the dough, because sourdough can be slower to rise than breads made only with packaged yeast. If you have the time for two risings, here's how: After you knead the dough, let it rise for 1 to 1 ½ hours, then punch it down, form into loaves and proceed as directed.*

*The monks at St. Bede also enjoy this bread baked as dinner rolls. Divide dough into 24 pieces; roll each piece into a ball. Place balls in lightly greased 18x12x1-inch pan. Let rise until doubled, then bake in a preheated 375-degree oven 15 to 20 minutes.*

# SOURDOUGH CRACKED WHEAT BREAD WITH SUNFLOWER SEEDS

Yield: 1 (2-pound) loaf.

## SPONGE:

$^1/_2$ cup **sourdough starter** (see conventional recipe, page 14)

$^1/_2$ cup **water**

1 cup **bread flour**

$^1/_2$ cup **whole wheat flour**

1 tablespoon **dark corn syrup**

## DOUGH:

$^1/_2$ cup **water**

1 tablespoon **dark corn syrup**

1 teaspoon **salt**

1 cup **bread flour**

$^1/_2$ cup **whole wheat flour**

$^1/_4$ cup **cracked wheat**

$^1/_4$ cup **unsalted sunflower seed kernels**

$^1/_8$ teaspoon **baking soda**

1 $^1/_2$ teaspoons **FLEISCHMANN'S Bread Machine Yeast**

**For sponge:** Combine sourdough starter, water, bread flour, whole wheat flour and corn syrup in large non-metallic bowl. Stir with a rubber scraper or plastic or wooden spoon until smooth. Cover bowl with plastic wrap. Let sponge develop at room temperature for 24 to 72 hours.

**For dough:** Place sponge, water, corn syrup, salt, bread flour, whole wheat flour, cracked wheat, sunflower kernels, baking soda and yeast in bread machine pan in the order suggested by manufacturer. Select **basic cycle; medium/normal color setting.**

# OVERNIGHT MULTIGRAIN WAFFLES

Yield: About 6 waffles.

## Bread Break

If I were making regular waffles, I'd use cake flour for a fluffy, more tender waffle. But I don't want to suggest that these heartier hotcakes are heavy or dense. You will be amazed how light and crisp a yeasted waffle can be, compared to the just-add-water boxed mixes. If you can't bear to wait until the next day to enjoy them, let the batter rise for at least one hour, then proceed as directed.

In this recipe, I've also reduced the amount of oil and eggs usually used for waffles to make them less fattening but no less flavorful. One morning I put out two stacks of waffles at the monastery breakfast table, each with a sign describing them. One read "Low-Fat Multigrain Waffles," and one was labeled "Regular High-Fat Waffles." Both stacks disappeared by the time breakfast was over.

| | |
|---|---|
| 1 package **FLEISCHMANN'S** **RapidRise Yeast** | 1 ¹/₂ cups **milk** |
| 1 ¹/₂ cups **all-purpose flour** | 1 tablespoon **barley malt syrup** or **dark corn syrup** |
| ¹/₄ cup **whole wheat flour** | 1 tablespoon **vegetable oil** |
| ¹/₄ cup **rye flour** | 2 **eggs** |
| 2 tablespoons **wheat germ** | 2 teaspoons **vanilla extract** |
| 1 teaspoon **salt** | |

Combine yeast, all-purpose flour, whole wheat flour, rye flour, wheat germ and salt in medium bowl; stir until thoroughly mixed. Combine milk, syrup and oil in small saucepan; heat to 120 to 130 degrees. Pour milk mixture into flour mixture; stir until batter is smooth. Cover bowl with plastic wrap and put in a cool place overnight. (If you like the taste of sourdough bread, as I do, just leave the covered bowl on the countertop.)

In the morning, stir batter down. Add eggs and vanilla; beat until thoroughly incorporated. If the batter seems a bit stiff, stir in 1 or 2 tablespoons milk at a time, until batter flows freely.

Preheat waffle iron and use batter according to manufacturer's instructions. (Some waffle irons hold more batter than others. This recipe makes 6 round waffles in mine.)

≈

*Note: Don't feel restricted to these flours. You could replace the rye with amaranth flour (a high-protein grain first grown by the Aztecs) or the whole wheat with spelt or kamut (similar-tasting ancient grains with less gluten). Try miller's bran or rolled oats instead of wheat germ, or crush some granola for a unique crunch.*

*When using flours other than all-purpose white, you might find you need to add a little more milk to make the batter pourable, because some grains absorb liquid faster than others.*

# No-Knead Oatmeal Rolls

Yield: 24 to 30 rolls.

1 ¹/₂ cups **rolled oats**

1 cup boiling **water**

2 packages **FLEISCHMANN'S Active Dry Yeast**

¹/₂ cup lukewarm **water**

2 cups lukewarm **milk**

¹/₂ cup **granulated sugar**

1 tablespoon **salt**

¹/₂ cup (1 stick) **butter**, melted

5 cups **all-purpose flour**

Additional **rolled oats**, for topping (optional)

Put oats in large bowl. Pour boiling water over oats; stir thoroughly. Let cool to lukewarm, about 30 minutes.

Sprinkle yeast over lukewarm water in small bowl; stir until dissolved. Let stand about 5 minutes, or until foamy. Add yeast mixture and milk to oats; stir until well mixed. Stir in sugar, salt and melted butter. Add flour, 1 cup at a time, stirring after each addition until flour is thoroughly incorporated. Cover bowl with a cloth and let rise in a warm, draft-free place 30 to 45 minutes, or until doubled.

Stir batter down and beat vigorously about 2 minutes. Spoon ¹/₄ cup batter into lightly greased muffin cups. If desired, sprinkle a few uncooked rolled oats on top of batter in each cup. Let stand about 15 minutes, or until batter rises to the top of each cup. While batter is rising, preheat oven to 400 degrees.

Bake rolls about 25 minutes, or until brown on top. Remove rolls from pans and let cool slightly on wire racks. Serve warm.

~

**Note:** *It really is important to stir the batter vigorously after the first rising to redistribute the yeast and make for an even texture in the roll. The outer crust of these rolls is thick and chewy because of the oats, but the interior is soft and fluffy.*

*If you don't have enough muffin tins or oven space to make all 30 rolls at once, you can divide the batter in half and refrigerate one portion while the first batch bakes. Then let the batter come to room temperature, stir it down again, and fill the muffin tins for a second batch.*

## Bread Break

Last year, the day before Thanksgiving I made a huge batch of oatmeal roll dough in our giant Hobart mixer. I invited five grade-school kids from a local parish to come make rolls for their Thanksgiving dinners. We had great fun forming the dough into different shapes: bowknots, fantans, cloverleafs, etc. They all left with homemade rolls for their families, and I had enough to feed the monks and more than 30 friends and family members who joined us for the meal. This recipe is a streamlined version of those rolls, formed as a thick batter instead of a kneaded dough.

# NINE-GRAIN BREAD

Yield: 2 loaves.

## Bread Break

This bread is among the all-time St. Bede Abbey favorites. My fellow monks devour it whenever it is served! It makes excellent toast at breakfast, serves as a hearty base for a sandwich of lunch meat and cheese, and goes well with just about any dinner entrée. Father Patrick in particular loves this bread and will go to the kitchen before supper to hunt down the slices remaining from lunch and take them to his place at table. I sit at the same table, and I'm pleased to report that he always shares the wealth!

I developed this recipe for Mike the Deli Guy to use as a base for the veggie stack sandwich at his shop. He would come over once a week or so and we'd bake about 16 loaves: 12 for him, 4 for the monks. The original recipe begins with "Pour 20 cups of warm water into the 50-quart bowl of the Hobart mixer."

### SPONGE:

1 cup lukewarm **water**

2 packages **FLEISCHMANN'S Active Dry Yeast**

1 cup **bread flour**

$^{1}/_{2}$ cup **whole wheat flour**

1 teaspoon **brown sugar**

### DOUGH:

1 $^{1}/_{2}$ cups lukewarm **water**

2 tablespoons **vegetable oil**

2 tablespoons **brown sugar**

2 teaspoons **salt**

1 cup **nine-grain cereal mix** (see note)

$^{1}/_{4}$ cup **millet**

$^{1}/_{4}$ cup **flaxseed**

4 $^{1}/_{4}$ to 5 cups **bread flour**, divided

**For sponge:** Combine water, yeast, bread flour, whole wheat flour and brown sugar in medium bowl; beat until smooth. Let stand 20 minutes, or until foamy and doubled in volume.

**For dough:** Add water, oil, brown sugar and salt to sponge; beat until smooth. Add cereal mix, millet and flaxseed; stir until thoroughly incorporated. Add 2 cups of the bread flour; beat until flour is thoroughly incorporated. Repeat with 2 cups bread flour. Add enough of the remaining bread flour, about $^{1}/_{4}$ cup at a time, to form a dough. Dough will be quite sticky, but resist the temptation to add too much more flour.

Turn out dough onto lightly floured surface. Knead 10 to 12 minutes. Rinse and dry the bowl, then oil surface of dough and place dough in bowl. Cover with a clean, dry cloth and let rise in a warm, draft-free place about 1 hour, or until doubled.

Punch down dough. Knead briefly to expel large air bubbles. Divide dough in half, then form each half into a loaf. Place loaves in lightly greased 9x5x3-inch loaf pans. Cover with a clean, dry cloth and let rise about 45 minutes, or until doubled.

About 15 minutes before end of rising time, preheat oven to 375 degrees. Bake loaves 40 to 45 minutes, or until loaves are golden brown, slide easily from the pan and sound hollow when tapped on the bottom. Let cool on wire racks.

~

**Note:** *The nine-grain cereal used for this bread is not the kind that you pour cold milk over. It's used to make hot cereal, such as oatmeal or porridge. You usually can find it in the bulk foods section of a large supermarket or health food store. It might be a blend of five or seven grains instead of nine. Whatever you find will work just dandy.*

# NINE-GRAIN BREAD

Bread Machine

Yield: 1 (1 ½-pound) loaf.

| | |
|---|---|
| 1 ¼ cups **water** | 2 tablespoons **millet** |
| 1 tablespoon **vegetable oil** | 2 tablespoons **flaxseed** |
| 1 teaspoon **salt** | 1 tablespoon **brown sugar** |
| 2 ½ cups **bread flour** | 2 teaspoons **FLEISCHMANN'S Bread Machine Yeast** |
| ½ cup **nine-grain cereal mix** | |
| ¼ cup **whole wheat flour** | |

Add water, oil, salt, bread flour, cereal mix, whole wheat flour, millet, flaxseed, brown sugar and yeast to bread machine pan in the order suggested by manufacturer. Select **basic/white; medium/normal color setting**.

~

# American Classics

Many of my fellow monks at St. Bede Abbey have studied or traveled in Europe and have come back with tales of hearty rolls served at monastery breakfasts, crusty loaves emerging from the oven of a tiny neighborhood *boulangerie*, and exquisite breads accompanying pasta dishes at a local trattoria. Father Ronald even brought me back an apron with pictures of breads from all over Italy: *cibatta, treccia, filone, pugliese, grissini,* et al.

Why hasn't somebody come up with an apron like that for the United States? Sure, a lot of our baking traditions came from European immigrants (New Orleans beignets and muffaletta come to mind), but what about Boston brown bread? Why not an apron with Parker House rolls, which have been around since the 1850s, or a sturdy loaf of anadama, which has been baked in this country since colonial times? Read the *Little House* books by Laura Ingalls Wilder, and you'll find the frontier origins of corn sticks—could there be anything more American? And while we're at it, let's feature a photo of hero sandwich bread (the hero sandwich being the alternative to that other American favorite, the hamburger) and arrange them all around a good old-fashioned loaf of basic white bread.

Don't get me wrong—I would like to sample French bread at a small café in the shadow of the Eiffel Tower just as much as the next Bread Head. But my explorations into the history of breads have led me not only all over the world, but all over my own country as well. I have come to appreciate the ingenuity of early American housewives (who would have thought that you could use cornmeal in so many different ways?) as much as the traditional methods of Old World bakers. In this chapter, you'll find recipes both old and new that reflect the unique culinary history of the United States.

# BOSTON BROWN BREAD

Yield: 2 loaves.

1/2 cup **raisins**

1/2 cup boiling **water**

1/2 cup **rye flour**

1/2 cup **cornmeal**

1/2 cup **all-purpose flour**

1 teaspoon **baking soda**

1/2 teaspoon **salt**

1/4 cup **molasses**

2 tablespoons **brown sugar**

1 cup lukewarm **buttermilk**

Boiling **water**

Remove labels from two empty 21-ounce cans (the kind that pie filling or fruit comes in); wash cans. Thoroughly grease the inside of the cans. Cut out 2 circles of waxed paper and place one in the bottom of each can.

Put raisins in a bowl; add 1/2 cup boiling water. Let stand 15 to 30 minutes to plump; drain well and pat dry with paper towels.

Combine rye flour, cornmeal, all-purpose flour, baking soda and salt in large bowl; stir until well mixed. In another bowl, combine molasses, brown sugar and lukewarm buttermilk; stir to mix. Pour buttermilk mixture into flour mixture; mix well. Fold in raisins until evenly distributed.

Divide batter evenly between the two prepared cans. Cover each can with greased aluminum foil and tie foil around the top with cotton string (or dental floss). Place a wire rack in the bottom of a large kettle with a lid. Place cans on rack. Pour in enough boiling water to come halfway up the sides of the cans. Cover kettle with lid; steam cans at a slow boil at least 2 hours, adding more water as needed. Bread is done when a wooden pick inserted in center comes out clean. Remove cans from water and remove the aluminum foil. Let bread cool to lukewarm before removing it from the cans. If bread resists coming out, run a thin knife blade around the inside of the can and gently shake out the bread.

## Bread Break

Boston brown bread is also called Third Bread because it uses one part each of three different grains. It is traditional to steam the bread in cans. Sometimes you see old-fashioned recipes that call for a one-pound lard bucket or a bread pudding mold, either of which would work if you happen to have one around! Whatever you use, just make sure that the cans are only half-filled with batter.

This is another bread that molasses lovers really enjoy. The small loaves that result from this recipe are dense and quite moist, so much so that you might suspect that they are underdone. But after two or three hours in a boiling water bath, you can rest assured that you've got it right.

Slice the bread thin and serve it with cream cheese and Baked Beans (page 120).

# PARKER HOUSE ROLLS

Yield: About 3 1/2 dozen.

## Bread Break

In 1854, the newly opened restaurant in the Parker House Hotel in Boston was under the leadership of a Frenchman named Sanzian. But it was a staff baker named Ward who is credited with the creation of the world-famous Parker House Rolls. Partly challenged by the prowess of executive chef Sanzian, Ward created a soft, crustless roll that caused quite a stir in mid-19th-century Boston society, because at the time, hard-crusted Vienna rolls were the style in upscale restaurants.

Parker House Roll has become part of the language, like Kleenex or Jell-O, and is used to describe any buttery roll that is folded over. But I obtained the original recipe from the accommodating staff at the hotel and received their generous permission to share it with my viewers. This is the real deal, Bread Heads—unless, of course, you dine at the Omni Parker House yourself!

6 cups **all-purpose flour**, divided

1/2 cup **granulated sugar**

2 teaspoons **salt**

2 packages **FLEISCHMANN'S Active Dry Yeast**

1 cup (2 sticks) **margarine** or **butter**, softened, divided

2 cups hot **tap water** (120 to 130 degrees)

1 **egg**

Combine 2 1/4 cups of the flour, sugar, salt and yeast in large bowl; stir to mix. Add 1/2 cup (1 stick) margarine. With electric mixer on low speed, gradually pour hot water into flour mixture. Add egg. Increase mixer speed to medium; beat 2 minutes, scraping bowl with rubber spatula. Beat in 3/4 cup of the flour, or enough to make a thick batter; continue beating 2 minutes, occasionally scraping bowl. With spoon, stir in enough of the remaining flour (about 2 1/2 cups) to make a soft dough.

Turn out dough onto lightly floured surface. Knead about 10 minutes, or until dough is smooth and elastic, working in remaining flour (about 1/2 cup) while kneading. Shape dough into a ball and place in large greased bowl; turn dough so top is greased. Cover with cloth and let rise in a warm, draft-free place about 1 1/2 hours, or until doubled. (Dough is doubled when two fingers pressed into dough leave a dent.)

Punch down dough by pushing down the center of dough with fist, then push edges of dough into center. Turn out dough onto lightly floured surface. Knead lightly to make smooth ball. Cover ball with bowl and let dough rest 15 minutes.

Put remaining 1/2 cup (1 stick) margarine in 18x12x1-inch baking pan. Place over low heat to melt margarine; tilt pan to grease bottom.

On lightly floured surface with floured rolling pin, roll dough 1/2-inch thick. With floured 2 3/4-inch round cutter, cut dough into circles. Holding dough circle by the edge, dip both sides into melted margarine in pan; fold in half. Arrange folded dough in rows in pan, each nearly touching the other. Knead trimmings together; reroll and cut more rolls. Cover rolls with a cloth and let rise about 40 minutes, or until doubled.

About 15 minutes before end of rising time, preheat oven to 400 degrees. Bake rolls 15 to 18 minutes, or until browned. Remove from pan and let cool slightly on wire racks. Serve warm.

# PARKER HOUSE ROLLS

Yield: 18 rolls.

| | |
|---|---|
| $^3/_4$ cup plus 2 tablespoons **water** | 3 cups **bread flour** |
| $^1/_4$ cup ($^1/_2$ stick) **butter** or **margarine** | $^1/_4$ cup **granulated sugar** |
| 1 **egg** | 2 teaspoons **FLEISCHMANN'S Bread Machine Yeast** |
| 1 teaspoon **salt** | $^1/_4$ cup ($^1/_2$ stick) **butter** or **margarine** |

Add water, $^1/_4$ cup butter, egg, salt, bread flour, sugar and yeast to bread machine pan in the order suggested by manufacturer. Select **dough/manual cycle**.

Meanwhile, put $^1/_4$ cup butter in jelly-roll pan. Melt butter over low heat. Tilt pan to grease bottom.

When cycle is complete, remove dough from machine to lightly floured surface. Roll out dough $^1/_2$-inch thick. With floured 2$^3/_4$-inch round cutter, cut dough into circles. Holding dough circle by the edge, dip both sides into melted butter in pan; fold in half. Arrange folded dough in rows in pan, each nearly touching the other. Knead trimmings together; reroll and cut more rolls. Cover and let rise in a warm, draft-free place about 45 minutes, or until doubled.

Bake in a preheated 400-degree oven 15 to 18 minutes, or until done. Remove from pan and let cool on wire rack.

# SINGLE LOAF WHITE BREAD

Yield: 1 loaf.

The milk in this recipe makes for a tender crumb on the bread, and the egg imparts a little extra richness, so this is a terrific all-purpose bread, just as good for special occasions as for every day.

This is a nice basic recipe for when you don't need two loaves of bread. Several other recipes in this cookbook are based on it, including Harvest Braid (page 54) and Braided Bread Bowl (page 30). I developed the recipe specifically for Housewarming Rolls (page 92).

Once you become more experienced, you can begin to experiment with variations on the dough itself. Try increasing the amount of sugar and using this dough for cinnamon rolls, or add a flavored oil or a tablespoon of herbs. Try adding some whole wheat flour or ¼ cup miller's bran for a heartier loaf.

1 package **FLEISCHMANN'S Active Dry Yeast**

1 ¼ cups lukewarm **milk**

1 tablespoon **granulated sugar**

1 **egg**

1 ½ teaspoons **salt**

1 tablespoon **vegetable oil**

3 to 3 ½ cups **bread flour**, divided

Sprinkle yeast over lukewarm milk in medium bowl; stir to dissolve. Add sugar, egg, salt and oil; stir to mix. Add 3 cups of the flour; beat well. Work in enough of the remaining flour to form a soft dough. Knead 6 to 8 minutes. Rinse and dry bowl, then oil surface of dough and place dough in bowl. Cover with a clean, dry cloth and let rise in a warm, draft-free place about 1 hour, or until doubled.

Punch down dough. Knead briefly to expel large air bubbles. Form into a loaf and place in lightly greased 9x5x3-inch loaf pan. Cover and let rise about 30 minutes, or until nearly doubled.

About 15 minutes before end of rising time, preheat oven to 375 degrees. Bake 35 to 40 minutes, or until bread slides easily from pan and sounds hollow when tapped on the bottom. Let cool on wire rack.

# SINGLE LOAF WHITE BREAD

Bread
Machine

Yield: 1 (2-pound) loaf.

$^1/_3$ cup **water**

1 cup **milk**

1 tablespoon **vegetable oil**

1 teaspoon **salt**

3 $^1/_4$ cups **bread flour**

1 tablespoon **granulated sugar**

2 teaspoons **FLEISCHMANN'S Bread Machine Yeast**

Add water, milk, oil, salt, bread flour, sugar and yeast to bread machine pan in the order suggested by manufacturer. Select **basic cycle; medium/normal color setting.**

# BRAIDED BREAD BOWL

Yield: 1 bread bowl.

*Bread Break*

This is a fairly easy recipe that, when successfully completed, always prompts the exclamation, "You made this?!" If you don't intend to eat the bowl, you can make it a day or two before a big party or buffet dinner. Make it a focal point of the table by placing it on a pedestal platter or a cloth-draped box. Depending on the size of your bowl, you might have a little dough left over. You can use this dough to make flowers or other decorative shapes to accent the serving platter for the main course or other dishes.

1 recipe **Single Loaf White Bread dough** (page 28)

1 **egg** beaten with 2 tablespoons **water**, for egg glaze

Prepare dough for Single Loaf White Bread through the first rising. Punch down dough and knead briefly to expel large air bubbles. Divide dough into 24 equal pieces. Roll each piece into a rope about 20 inches long. Twist 2 ropes together; pinch ends to seal. Repeat with remaining ropes.

Invert a 3- or 4-quart ovenproof mixing bowl onto a lightly greased baking sheet. Heavily grease outside of bowl. Starting at rim of bowl, wrap twists around bowl, pinching ends to join each new twist to the previous one. If the dough seems a bit dry, lightly brush the previous layer with water before adding the next twist. Continue wrapping twists until entire bowl is covered. Cover with a cloth and let rise in a warm, draft-free place about 15 minutes. Meanwhile, preheat oven to 375 degrees.

Brush dough with egg glaze. Bake 25 to 30 minutes, or until crust is rich brown and firm to the touch. Let bread cool on bowl 15 minutes. Gently remove bread from bowl. Cover bowl with fluffy towel; gently replace bread and let cool completely.

Use braided bread bowl as a serving bowl or centerpiece. Line braided bread bowl with a decorative towel or napkin and fill with small rolls or fresh fruit.

*Note: If the surface of the bread bowl seems to be browning too quickly, lightly cover it with aluminum foil. I find that the top few coils tend to brown more quickly and usually need protection. If the heat of the oven causes the top few coils (which actually form the bottom of the bowl) to spring up or become distorted, use a plate to flatten them so you'll have a basket that sits level on the table.*

# Corn Sticks

Yield: 12 to 14 corn sticks.

| | |
|---|---|
| 2 cups **yellow cornmeal** | $^1/_2$ teaspoon **salt** |
| $^1/_4$ cup **brown sugar** | 1 cup **sour cream** |
| 1 teaspoon **baking powder** | 1 **egg** |
| $^1/_2$ teaspoon **baking soda** | |

Generously grease two corn stick pans; be sure to also grease the top of the pans because batter tends to escape the mold somewhat. Place pans in oven and preheat oven to 400 degrees.

Combine cornmeal, brown sugar, baking powder, baking soda and salt in medium bowl; stir until thoroughly mixed. Combine sour cream and egg in small bowl; beat until smooth. Add egg mixture to cornmeal mixture; stir until just moistened. Do not overmix.

Remove preheated pans from oven and fill molds with batter to just below the top of the pan. Return to 400-degree oven and bake 20 minutes, or until golden brown on top. Remove corn sticks from pans and let cool briefly on wire racks. Serve warm.

*Note: When testing this recipe, my students and I created a version that substituted $^1/_4$ cup maple-flavored syrup for the brown sugar, and added $^1/_2$ teaspoon maple flavoring. The resulting corn sticks had a subtle maple flavor and were delicious topped with butter. My young friend Chris prefers them this way, and I include the variation at his insistence.*

*Corn sticks make a delicious accompaniment to hot cereal in the morning, can add variety to a soup-and-salad lunch, and make an attractive display on a Thanksgiving buffet with turkey and giblet gravy. My buddy Mike the Deli Guy likes them with ranch dressing and salsa, and thinks they belong alongside a bowl of chili or a taco salad.*

## Bread Break

In the early 1800s, people in the Midwest often ate corn dodger, which was made of cornmeal, sour milk and a little bacon grease. The dough was shaped into patties or little ears of corn and cooked in a skillet, or wrapped in corn husks and baked in the embers of the fire. Later, cast-iron pans were produced with molds shaped like ears of corn. These molds are still available today. Before you buy one, check the quality of the mold impression—there are cheap models out there that work fine but make only a rough image of a corn ear. You can find antique molds that cost anywhere from $50 to $100 in antique shops and malls. These antiques are still usable, but so are new models of the same quality that can be had for about $20. Glass corn stick molds are more rare, but work well and are worth the extra effort to hunt for them.

# Anadama Bread

Yield: 1 large loaf.

## Bread Break

I have read several different versions of the story of how this bread got its name, but they all revolve around the idea of a disgruntled husband with a wife named Ana. In some versions, he has to make his own bread because she's so inept, in others he's tired of plain white bread and develops his own recipe for the sake of variety. In every story, he mutters, "Ana, damn her! Ana, damn her!" as he kneads the dough. But somewhere I have read another explanation that seems just as plausible: that "anadama" is a variety of corn. Unfortunately, a look in the *Oxford English Dictionary* yielded no results, and Webster's didn't help either, so I'll have to keep looking for a definitive answer. But don't wait for me to complete my research before you make this bread, especially if you like the flavor of molasses.

This bread doesn't last more than a day in the monastery, with Brother Anthony and Father James coming back to the kitchen for a slice as an

---

³/₄ cup **cornmeal**

1 cup boiling **water**

¹/₄ cup **molasses**

3 tablespoons **solid vegetable shortening** or **butter**

1 ¹/₂ teaspoons **salt**

1 package **FLEISCHMANN'S Active Dry Yeast**

¹/₄ cup lukewarm **water**

3 ¹/₂ to 4 ¹/₄ cups **bread flour**, divided

---

Combine cornmeal, boiling water, molasses, shortening and salt in a medium bowl; stir until thoroughly mixed. Let cool to lukewarm. Dissolve yeast in lukewarm water; let stand until foamy. Stir yeast mixture into cornmeal mixture. Add 3 cups of the flour, 1 cup at a time, stirring after each addition until flour is thoroughly incorporated. Add enough of the remaining flour to make a soft dough.

Turn out dough onto a lightly floured surface. Knead 8 to 10 minutes, adding small amounts of flour as needed to keep the dough from sticking to the work surface. Rinse and dry the bowl, then oil the surface of the dough and place in the bowl. Cover with a clean, dry cloth and let rise in a warm, draft-free place about 1 hour, or until doubled.

Punch down dough. Form dough into a loaf. Place in a lightly greased 9x5x3-inch loaf pan. Cover and let rise about 45 minutes, or until nearly doubled. About 15 minutes before end of rising time, preheat oven to 375 degrees. Bake loaf 40 to 45 minutes, or until dark brown. Bread is done when it slides easily from the pan and sounds hollow when tapped on the bottom. Remove from pan and let cool on wire rack.

**Note:** *Normally I prefer to bake bread in a medium, 8¹/₂ x 4¹/₂ x 2¹/₂-inch loaf pan. But this recipe makes just a little too much dough for that size pan, and the resulting loaf can appear misshapen and is prone to be a bit doughy in the center. The larger, 9x5x3-inch pan is a better fit. If you don't have that size pan, just divide the dough in half and make two free-form loaves on a single baking sheet.*

afternoon snack. I like to put it out at breakfast because it makes excellent toast.

# ANADAMA BREAD

Yield: 1 (2-pound) loaf.

1 ¹/₄ cups plus 2 tablespoons
  **water**

3 tablespoons **molasses**

2 ¹/₂ tablespoons **butter** or
  **margarine**

1 ¹/₄ teaspoons **salt**

3 cups **bread flour**

²/₃ cup **cornmeal**

2 teaspoons
  **FLEISCHMANN'S Bread
  Machine Yeast**

Add water, molasses, butter, salt, bread flour, cornmeal and yeast to bread machine pan in the order suggested by manufacturer. Select **basic cycle; light/normal color setting**.

# HERO SANDWICH BREAD

Yield: 2 long or 4 short loaves.

## Bread Break

As far as I'm concerned, the best hero sandwich is the Gondola made at Avanti's in Peoria, Illinois, which was one of our favorite hangout places after high school football and basketball games. Avanti's bread is legendary in central Illinois, and the recipe is a well-kept secret. I have seen several different pirated versions of it, but as is so often the case, nothing you can produce in your kitchen can equal the real thing. Here's my modest attempt, which I have developed after extensive experimentation, the samples of which were eagerly devoured by the stage crew of our Academy theater department. Thinly sliced salami, boiled ham, American cheese and lettuce are the classic Gondola toppings, but just about anything you put on this bread will be delicious.

I serve sandwiches made with this bread every year at my "Opening Day of Baseball" party. I invite alumni, students and friends, make piles of sandwiches and put soda on ice, then reserve the

2 packages **FLEISCHMANN'S Active Dry Yeast**

1 ¹/₂ cups lukewarm **water**

¹/₂ cup **granulated sugar**

3 tablespoons **vegetable oil**

2 teaspoons **salt**

1 **egg**

5 to 6 cups **all-purpose flour**, divided

Dissolve yeast in lukewarm water in large bowl. Add sugar, oil, salt and egg; mix well. Add 5 cups of the flour, 1 cup at a time, mixing well after each addition. Turn dough out onto lightly floured surface. Knead 5 to 8 minutes, adding as much of the remaining flour as needed to make a fairly soft dough. Rinse and dry bowl, then oil bowl. Put dough in oiled bowl and turn dough to coat with oil. Cover and let rise in a warm, draft-free place about 1 hour, or until doubled.

Punch down dough. Knead briefly. Cover and let rise 45 minutes. Punch down dough. Knead again briefly. Divide dough into 2 or 4 pieces; form into two long loaves, slightly flattened, or four short loaves. Place loaves on lightly greased 18x12x1-inch baking pan. Cover with a cloth and let rise about 30 minutes, or until almost doubled.

About 15 minutes before end of rising time, preheat oven to 350 degrees. Bake loaves 30 to 35 minutes, or until loaves sound hollow when tapped. Remove from baking pan and let cool on wire racks.

*Note: An 18x12x1-inch pan (also called a half sheet) is a commercial pan that may be hard to find in the kitchen aisle of the average supermarket. Use two 15x10x1-inch jelly-roll pans if necessary to accommodate four loaves.*

*Because of the relatively large amount of sugar, this bread will darken more quickly than other breads, so keep a careful eye on it during baking and rotate the pans to prevent uneven browning, especially if your oven is hotter near the back than in the front, as mine is. The crust will be fairly thin, and the texture will be very fine and quite soft because of the egg. Be sure to knead the dough thoroughly, so that the bread will hold together under the pressure of the sandwich fillings.*

*This recipe can be doubled or even tripled, but you'll need a large mixer with a sturdy dough hook to knead it adequately.*

school's AV room with the big-screen TV as our meeting place. It doesn't matter who's playing—when you're starved for baseball after the long winter of NBA and NHL, any baseball is worthwhile if you have the right refreshments.

# HERO SANDWICH BREAD

Yield: 1 loaf.

$^3/_4$ cup plus 2 tablespoons **water**

1 tablespoon plus 1 $^1/_2$ teaspoons **vegetable oil**

1 **egg**

1 teaspoon **salt**

3 cups **bread flour**

$^1/_4$ cup **granulated sugar**

1 $^1/_2$ teaspoons **FLEISCHMANN'S Bread Machine Yeast**

Add water, oil, egg, salt, bread flour, sugar and yeast to bread machine pan in the order suggested by manufacturer. Select **dough/manual cycle**.

When cycle is complete, remove dough from machine. Shape into long loaf, about 16 inches; flatten slightly. Place on greased baking sheet. Cover and let rise in a warm, draft-free place about 45 minutes, or until almost doubled.

Bake in a preheated 350-degree oven about 25 minutes, or until done. Remove from sheet and let cool on wire rack.

# Texas Moppin' Rolls

Yield: 12 rolls.

## Bread Break

Most recipes for rolls use milk to make a softer, more tender crumb, but I used water in this recipe because I wanted these rolls to be sturdy enough to stand up to a Texas-sized slice of Barbecued Beef Brisket (page 118). You can even slice them to make buffet sandwiches, as I have done for our community night card parties. The spicy taste contrasts nicely with a sweet barbecue sauce, and there's nothing better for moppin' up the last of the Baked Beans (page 120) on your plate. If you want daintier rolls, you can divide the dough into 16 or even 20 pieces, but then everyone's going to take two anyway, so you might as well make them large!

2 packages **FLEISCHMANN'S Active Dry Yeast**

1 teaspoon **honey**

2 cups lukewarm **water**

1 teaspoon **salt**

1 1/2 teaspoons **crushed red pepper**

1/2 cup minced **onion**

1 cup shredded **Monterey Jack cheese**

1/2 cup shredded **Cheddar cheese**

6 1/2 to 7 cups **all-purpose flour**, divided

Combine yeast, honey and lukewarm water in large bowl; stir until completely dissolved. Add salt, hot red pepper flakes, onion, Monterey Jack cheese and Cheddar cheese; stir until thoroughly mixed. Add 6 cups of the flour, 2 cups at a time, mixing after each addition until the flour is completely incorporated.

Turn out dough onto a lightly floured surface. Knead 6 to 8 minutes, adding enough of remaining flour to form a fairly stiff dough. Rinse and dry the bowl, then oil surface of dough and place dough in bowl. Cover with a clean, dry cloth and let rise in a warm, draft-free place about 1 hour, or until doubled.

Punch down dough. Knead briefly to expel large air bubbles. Divide dough into 12 equal pieces. Roll each piece into a fat oval. Place rolls in a lightly greased 13x9x2-inch baking pan (three rolls across, four down). Let rise about 20 minutes, or until nearly doubled.

While rolls are rising, preheat oven to 375 degrees. Place on middle rack of oven and bake 35 to 40 minutes, or until top crust is browned. Remove rolls from pan and let cool on racks.

**Note:** *With so many different palates to please, our abbey cooks are usually pretty cautious about spicy seasonings. As a result, sometimes monastery food is a bit bland, so I like to create breads with strong flavors. Every time I serve these rolls, one of the brothers is sure to com-*

ment on how he expected "just another roll" and got a mouthful of pep-per-and-cheese-bread-with-an-attitude. These rolls are actually pretty mild compared to a lot of Tex-Mex food, so feel free to increase the amount of crushed red pepper.

I used ordinary dried crushed red pepper (hot red pepper flakes) for this recipe, but if you keep fresh jalapenos or other hot peppers in the fridge, by all means use them. Three 3-inch jalapenos, minced fine, pro-vide moderate heat. You can experiment with other peppers as well.

# TEXAS MOPPIN' ROLLS

Yield: 6 rolls.

1 cup plus 3 tablespoons **water**

$^1/_2$ teaspoon **honey**

$^1/_2$ teaspoon **salt**

3 cups **bread flour**

$^1/_2$ cup shredded **Monterey Jack cheese**

$^1/_4$ cup shredded **Cheddar cheese**

$^1/_4$ cup **minced onion**

$^3/_4$ teaspoon **crushed red pepper**

1 $^1/_2$ teaspoons **FLEISCHMANN'S Bread Machine Yeast**

Add water, honey, salt, bread flour, Monterey Jack cheese, Cheddar cheese, onion, hot red pepper flakes and yeast to bread machine pan in the order suggested by manufacturer. Select **dough/manual cycle.**

When cycle is complete, remove dough from machine. Cover and let rest 10 minutes. Divide dough into 6 equal pieces. Roll each piece into an oval. Place rolls in greased 9x9-inch square baking pan. Cover and let rise in a warm, draft-free place about 30 minutes, or until almost doubled.

Bake in a preheated 375-degree oven 20 minutes, or until done. Remove from pan and let cool on wire rack.

# DELIGHTS OF CHOCOLATE

I'm sure that I will be denounced as a kitchen-cabinet heretic by the statement I'm about to make, but I think there is entirely too much chocolate out there.

(You could actually hear my ratings scream as they suddenly plummeted several points, couldn't you?)

People put chocolate in everything these days: from cocktails to coffee to pancakes to soup to gravy to chili. I entered "chocolate recipes" into an Internet search engine and got over 5 million sites. On one Web site I found nine different recipes called "Death by Chocolate"—just how much does it take to kill you? I found a chocolate-flavored alcoholic beverage called an "Irish Car Bomb," which is not only in questionable taste, but is also further proof of the cocoa bean's violent takeover of the culinary world.

So why am I presenting a chapter of chocolate breads? I have two very good reasons. The first is that I genuinely like the taste of chocolate, and there are some breads that really benefit from that flavor. Doughnuts come to mind, of course, and muffins. You'd be surprised how rye bread benefits from a little cocoa powder and a tablespoon of instant coffee. Chocolate and raspberry preserves go together in Norfolk scones like cinnamon goes with apples. And chocolate bread pudding? The transformation from stale baguette to warm-and-chocolatey-custard-like-dessert will make you leave bread out on the counter overnight on purpose.

See, I'm not against chocolate. I just believe in proportion, balance, moderation—it's a monk thing. Desserts that use three different kinds of chocolate plus a fudge sauce just don't appeal to me; they lack focus, somehow, and seem to pummel the palate instead of caressing it with cocoa. I'm also opposed to chocolate recipes that use too much sugar, and you might notice the relatively small proportion of sugar in some of the recipes that follow.

And the second reason I have a chapter devoted to chocolate breads? My sister the chocolate lover keeps sending me threatening e-mails.

# CHOCOLATE BREAD PUDDING

Yield: 6 to 8 servings.

4 (1-ounce) squares
  **semisweet chocolate**

2 cups **whole milk**

$1/4$ cup **granulated sugar**

2 **eggs**, beaten

2 teaspoons **vanilla extract**

4 cups cubed **stale bread**
  (1-inch cubes, crusts
  removed)

$1/2$ cup **toffee bits**

2 tablespoons **butter**, cut into
  small pieces

**For garnish:**

Whipped cream

Additional toffee bits

Break chocolate into small pieces, then chop fine, using a sharp, sturdy knife or a food processor fitted with steel blade. Combine milk, sugar and chocolate in large saucepan; heat over low heat 15 to 20 minutes, stirring constantly, or until chocolate is completely melted. Do not allow to boil. Remove from heat and let cool to lukewarm.

Add eggs and vanilla (yes, right there in the saucepan—no need to dirty a bowl!) and stir until mixed. Add bread cubes; stir to coat. Let stand 30 minutes, stirring occasionally, until bread cubes are thoroughly soaked. Stir in toffee bits. Transfer mixture to a lightly greased 1 $1/2$-quart glass baking dish. Dot surface with butter.

Bake on middle rack of preheated 350-degree oven 45 minutes, or until knife inserted in center comes out clean. Let cool slightly. Serve warm, topped with whipped cream and sprinkled with toffee bits.

❧

*Note: Be sure to finely chop the chocolate so it will melt quickly and evenly. Also, don't let the chocolate overheat in the milk mixture; 120 degrees is hot enough to melt the chocolate without scorching it. The mixture should be stirred constantly.*

*I do not recommend ordinary commercial sandwich bread for this pudding. Use something more substantial, such as stale French Baguettes (page 107). Brioche also makes an excellent bread pudding.*

*The toffee bits add some extra sweetness, but they melt completely during baking. I recommend using a few as garnish on the whipped cream. The combination of the smooth pudding and the crunchy toffee is delightful.*

## Bread Break

Usually I don't much care for custard-like desserts, but this chocolate bread pudding is an exception—and a truly exceptional recipe it is! The first time I made it, I fell in love. It's easy, low-tech (doesn't use fancy tools, ingredients or methods) and is absolutely delicious served warm. If you are a chocolate lover, the yield should read: "one to eight servings."

# BAKED CHOCOLATE DOUGHNUTS

Yield: 12 to 14 doughnuts plus doughnut holes.

Whenever I have made these doughnuts for the brethren, there are always a few left over after breakfast. The doughnuts mysteriously disappear as confreres take their morning coffee breaks. By lunch, nothing is left but crumbs—always a pleasure for the baker to see!

2 ³/₄ cups **all-purpose flour,** divided

3 tablespoons **unsweetened cocoa powder**

¹/₄ teaspoon **salt**

1 package **FLEISCHMANN'S RapidRise Yeast**

1 cup **milk**

2 tablespoons **butter**

¹/₂ cup **granulated sugar**

1 **egg,** beaten

¹/₂ cup **miniature semisweet chocolate morsels** (or milk chocolate morsels)

Combine 1 ³/₄ cups of the flour, cocoa powder, salt and yeast in medium bowl; stir until thoroughly mixed. Combine milk, butter and sugar in small saucepan; heat to 120 to 130 degrees. Pour milk mixture into flour mixture; stir 2 minutes. Stir in egg. Add the remaining 1 cup flour; stir until thoroughly incorporated. Dough will be quite moist and sticky. Stir in chocolate morsels. Cover dough with damp cloth; let rest 10 minutes.

Line two 15x10x1-inch jelly-roll pans with parchment paper or aluminum foil. Heavily flour rolling pin and work surface. Roll out dough ¹/₂-inch thick. Cut out doughnuts using a doughnut cutter or two biscuit cutters. Place doughnuts on one pan, doughnut holes on the other. Let rise in a warm, draft-free place 45 minutes, or until doubled.

About 15 minutes before end of rising time, preheat oven to 350 degrees. Bake doughnuts 15 to 20 minutes; slightly less time for doughnut holes. Remove from pans and let cool briefly on wire rack.

If desired, frost doughnuts with Chocolate Buttercream Frosting (page 45).

*Note: In all honesty, these are not quite as good as doughnuts fried in oil, but the chocolate flavor is so good, you won't mind. The one difficulty I discovered was that if your baking pans are darkened from years of use, the bottoms of the doughnuts can burn easily. That's why the directions say to line the pans with parchment paper or aluminum foil. If your pans are shiny and new, you should have no problem.*

# BAKED CHOCOLATE DOUGHNUTS

Yield: 15 doughnuts.

$^1/_2$ cup **water**

$^1/_2$ cup **milk**

2 tablespoons **butter** or **margarine**

1 **egg**

$^1/_4$ teaspoon **salt**

3 cups plus 3 tablespoons **bread flour**

$^1/_4$ cup **unsweetened cocoa powder**

$^1/_2$ cup **granulated sugar**

2 teaspoons **FLEISCHMANN'S Bread Machine Yeast**

$^1/_2$ cup **miniature semisweet chocolate morsels**

Add water, milk, butter, egg, salt, bread flour, cocoa powder, sugar and yeast to bread machine pan in the order suggested by manufacturer. Select **dough/manual cycle**.

When cycle is complete, remove dough from machine. Knead in chocolate morsels until evenly distributed. Cover and let rest 10 minutes.

Roll out dough on lightly floured surface to $^1/_2$-inch thickness. Cut with floured 3-inch doughnut cutter. Place on greased baking sheet. Cover and let rise in a warm, draft-free place about 45 minutes, or until doubled.

Bake in a preheated 350-degree oven 15 to 18 minutes, or until done. Remove from baking sheet and let cool on wire rack.

If desired, frost doughnuts with Chocolate Buttercream Frosting (page 45).

# CHOCOLATE BUTTERMILK SCONES WITH RASPBERRY FILLING

Yield: 8 servings.

## Bread Break

This is my all-time favorite "instant hospitality" recipe. If a friend calls and says, "Let's meet for coffee. I'll be over in half an hour," I know I can start this recipe and the scones will be coming out of the oven just as my guest arrives. I once worked on a pledge drive in Milwaukee and made these live on camera in an unfamiliar kitchen set, then served them to the volunteers as they were answering phones. So you should have no trouble making them at home.

My buddy Greg made the (slightly exaggerated) comment: "These are so light and so good that you could eat them until you were violently ill, and you wouldn't really mind." The lightness comes from using buttermilk instead of heavy cream, a suggestion I received from a viewer to whom I owe my thanks. I have even made these with powdered buttermilk (look

2 cups **all-purpose flour**

¹⁄₄ cup **unsweetened cocoa powder**

¹⁄₂ cup **granulated sugar**

1 tablespoon **baking powder**

¹⁄₈ teaspoon **baking soda**

¹⁄₄ teaspoon **salt**

¹⁄₂ cup (1 stick) **butter**, cold, cut into small pieces

¹⁄₃ cup **milk chocolate morsels**, chopped fine

¹⁄₂ cup **buttermilk**

1 **egg**, beaten

¹⁄₂ cup **raspberry preserves**

Sift flour, cocoa powder, sugar, baking powder, baking soda and salt into large bowl; stir to mix well. Using a pastry blender or two sharp knives, cut butter into flour mixture until mixture resembles coarse crumbs. Stir in finely chopped chocolate. Combine buttermilk and egg in small bowl; whisk until well blended. Pour into flour mixture; stir with a wooden spoon until just moistened. Do not overmix.

Turn out dough onto a lightly floured surface; knead gently 8 or 10 strokes. Divide dough in half. On lightly floured surface, pat each piece into a flattened 8-inch round. Place one round on lightly greased baking sheet or jelly-roll pan. Spread raspberry preserves on top of round. Place second round on top of preserves. Using a large knife or metal spatula, cut into 8 wedges, wiping knife after each cut.

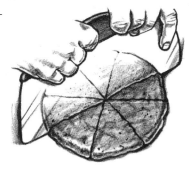

Bake in a preheated 400-degree oven 15 to 20 minutes, or until firm on the edges but still slightly soft in

44

the middle. Let cool on a wire rack, then cut wedges apart before serving.

≈

**Note:** *Chop the chocolate morsels in an electric blender or food processor, if you have one. The chocolate should be granular rather than powdered. If it's a hot day, put the chocolate morsels in the freezer to firm up before chopping, or you'll end up with a gooey mess!*

*A scone with a layer of filling is sometimes called a Norfolk scone, although I have yet to see a satisfactory explanation for the appellation. You can substitute strawberry preserves for raspberry preserves.*

in the same grocery aisle as nonfat dry milk powder) and they turned out just as light and delicious as the ones made with the fresh product.

## CHOCOLATE BUTTERCREAM FROSTING

Yield: About 2 cups.

| | |
|---|---|
| 1 cup **semisweet chocolate chunks** or **morsels** | ¹/₃ cup **heavy** or **whipping cream** |
| 2 tablespoons **butter** | 3 cups sifted **confectioners' sugar** |

Combine chocolate, butter and cream in saucepan or microwave-safe bowl. Heat on stovetop or in microwave oven until ingredients melt and blend together when stirred. Stir in confectioners' sugar, ¹/₂ cup at a time, until you achieve a thick but spreadable consistency. If necessary, add additional confectioners' sugar to thicken or additional cream (or milk) to thin.

Use to frost Baked Chocolate Doughnuts (page 42), if desired.

≈

# CHOCOLATE CHUNK BREAD

Yield: 1 loaf; about 12 servings.

## Bread Break

This bread is for those who prefer dark chocolate, especially for those who find most chocolate breads and muffins too sweet. With only ¼ cup sugar in the dough, the bread gets its sweetness from the chunks of chocolate kneaded into the dough. Milk chocolate could be substituted for the semisweet chocolate, but try it this way first and see if you don't appreciate the deep chocolate flavor.

Using a baking dish for this bread rather than a rectangular pan makes a smooth, round loaf that yields an attractive addition to the breakfast table. Given the fact that I have never had any leftovers, I suspect my fellow monks would eat it no matter what shape I baked it in.

1 package **FLEISCHMANN'S RapidRise Yeast**

3 tablespoons **unsweetened cocoa powder**

1 teaspoon **salt**

2 ½ cups **bread flour**, divided

1 cup **milk**

¼ cup **granulated sugar**

1 tablespoon **butter**

3 (1-ounce) squares **semisweet chocolate**, coarsely chopped

Combine yeast, cocoa powder, salt and 1 ½ cups of the flour in a large bowl; stir to mix. Combine milk, sugar and butter in a small saucepan; heat to 120 to 130 degrees, stirring occasionally. Pour milk mixture into flour mixture; beat until smooth. Add the remaining 1 cup flour, about ¼ cup at a time, mixing until flour is completely incorporated. The dough will be quite soft and sticky.

Using a plastic dough scraper in one hand, knead the dough 5 minutes; keep the other hand dusted with additional flour to facilitate kneading. Cover dough and let rest 10 minutes.

Flatten dough. Place chopped chocolate on top. Fold sides of dough up over chocolate. Knead to distribute chocolate evenly throughout the dough. Dust your hands with additional cocoa powder and shape the dough into a round ball. Place ball of dough in a lightly greased 1 ½-quart round baking dish. Cover with a dry cloth. Let rise in a warm, draft-free place about 1 hour, or until nearly doubled.

About 15 minutes before end of rising time, preheat oven to 350 degrees. Place bread in the middle third of the oven and bake 35 to 40 minutes, or until sides are browned and loaf sounds hollow when tapped on the bottom. If the top crust seems to be browning too quickly, cover loosely with foil the last 10 minutes of baking. Remove bread from baking dish and let cool on wire rack.

**Note:** *For many breads, I prefer to use active dry yeast with the traditional two or three risings because I find that the flavor and texture are more complex. But with the strong dark chocolate dominating this loaf, fast-rising yeast works just as well, without sacrificing taste.*

*Most people probably own a 1 1/2-quart baking dish, so that's what I've specified here. But I generally use the 1-quart size because it makes a loaf of bread that is almost perfectly round, so use that size if you have it. You can also bake this bread on a pie plate with good results. It's also worth noting that this recipe works well with all-purpose flour, although you may need to add slightly more flour when using all-purpose.*

# Chocolate Chunk Bread

Yield: 1 loaf.

3/4 cup **milk**

1/4 cup plus 1 tablespoon **water**

1 tablespoon **butter**

1 teaspoon **salt**

2 1/2 cups **bread flour**

1/4 cup **granulated sugar**

3 tablespoons **unsweetened cocoa powder**

1 1/2 teaspoons **FLEISCHMANN'S Bread Machine Yeast**

3 (1-ounce) squares **semisweet chocolate**, coarsely chopped

Add milk, water, butter, salt, bread flour, sugar, cocoa powder and yeast to bread machine pan in the order suggested by manufacturer. Select **dough/manual cycle.**

When cycle is complete, remove dough from machine to lightly floured surface. Cover and let rest 10 minutes. Flatten dough. Place chopped chocolate on top. Fold up sides of dough. Knead to distribute chocolate evenly throughout dough. Shape dough into a ball. Place in greased 1 1/2-quart baking dish. Cover and let rise in a warm, draft-free place about 1 hour, or until doubled.

Bake in a preheated 350-degree oven 40 minutes, or until done. Remove from baking dish and let cool on wire rack.

# HONEY MOCHA BREAD

Yield: 2 loaves.

## Bread Break

As regular viewers of the program know, I don't much care for the taste of caraway seeds. But I'm a big fan of rye flour (I even add a little to my pizza dough on occasion), and I prefer honey over any other sweetener. I developed this recipe for a bread that uses rye flour and honey, along with two other favorite flavors of mine, cocoa and coffee. The result is this dark loaf with a light texture that goes with just about any hearty meal, but especially well with beef dishes. The mocha flavor is quite subtle, so don't be expecting something like mocha almond fudge ice cream or gourmet coffee.

2 packages **FLEISCHMANN'S Active Dry Yeast**

1 cup lukewarm **water**

$^1/_2$ cup **honey**

1 cup lukewarm **milk**

1 cup **rye flour**

$^1/_4$ cup **unsweetened cocoa powder**

1 tablespoon **instant coffee granules**

2 tablespoons **vegetable oil**

2 teaspoons **salt**

4 $^1/_2$ to 5 cups **bread flour**, divided

Combine yeast, lukewarm water and honey in large bowl; stir until yeast is completely dissolved. Add milk, rye flour, cocoa powder, coffee granules, oil and salt; stir until thoroughly mixed. Add 4 cups of the bread flour, 1 cup at a time, mixing after each addition until flour is completely incorporated.

Turn out dough onto lightly floured surface. Knead, adding small amounts of the remaining bread flour as needed to keep the dough manageable. Both the honey and the rye flour will make the dough sticky, so be careful not to add too much flour. Occasionally, as needed, scrape up any dough sticking to the counter and knead it in. Knead 10 to 12 minutes, or until you have a slightly stiff dough. Rinse and dry bowl, then oil surface of dough and place dough in bowl. Cover with a clean, dry cloth and let rise in a warm, draft-free place 60 to 75 minutes, or until doubled.

Punch down dough. Let dough rest 5 minutes. Divide dough into two equal pieces. Form each piece into a fat oval. Place both loaves on a lightly greased baking sheet. (You can sprinkle a little cornmeal on the baking sheet if you like that kind of bottom crust.) Cover and let rise 30 to 45 minutes, or until nearly doubled.

About 15 minutes before end of rising time, preheat oven to 350 degrees. Place loaves in lower third of oven and bake 30 to 35 minutes, or until crust is dark brown and loaf sounds hollow when tapped on the bottom. If loaves seem to be darkening too quickly, lightly cover them with aluminum foil until the last 5 to 10 minutes of baking. Remove from baking sheet and let cool on wire rack.

≈

*Note: You will almost certainly have to cover the loaves with foil for part of the baking time, because the honey in the dough makes them brown quickly. You can bake these loaves in medium loaf pans (8 1/2 x 4 1/2 x 2 1/2 inches), but I like free-form loaves better. For rolls, form dough into 24 balls and place balls in muffin tins to rise; bake 15 to 20 minutes.*

# HONEY MOCHA BREAD

Yield: 1 loaf.

1/2 cup **water**

1/2 cup **milk**

1/4 cup **honey**

1 tablespoon **vegetable oil**

1 teaspoon **salt**

2 1/4 cups **bread flour**

1/2 cup **rye flour**

2 tablespoons **unsweetened cocoa powder**

1 1/2 teaspoons **instant coffee granules**

2 teaspoons **FLEISCHMANN'S Bread Machine Yeast**

Add water, milk, honey, oil, salt, bread flour, rye flour, cocoa powder, coffee granules and yeast to bread machine pan in the order suggested by manufacturer. Select **dough/manual cycle**.

When cycle is complete, remove dough from machine. With lightly floured hands, shape dough into an oval. Place on greased baking sheet. Cover and let rise in a warm, draft-free place about 1 hour, or until doubled.

Bake in preheated 350-degree oven 25 to 30 minutes, or until done. Remove from baking sheet and let cool on wire rack.

≈

# CHOCOLATE MINT MUFFINS

Yield: 12 muffins.

## Bread Break

Mint is the herb of refreshment, so these Chocolate Mint Muffins are a perfect gift for a friend or co-worker who's having a rough week. Or, use them as a way to say "Congratulations!" to a family member who's just finished a big job, like cleaning out the attic or painting the garage. When served warm from the oven, these minty muffins cry out for cold milk or good coffee.

1 ¹/₂ cups **all-purpose flour**

¹/₂ cup **granulated sugar**

¹/₄ cup **unsweetened cocoa powder**

1 tablespoon **baking powder**

¹/₄ teaspoon **salt**

1 **egg**, beaten

1 cup **milk**

¹/₄ cup (¹/₂ stick) **butter**, melted

28 **crème de menthe thin candies**, chopped

Sift flour, sugar, cocoa powder, baking powder and salt into medium bowl; stir to mix. In another bowl, combine egg, milk and butter; beat to mix well. Pour egg mixture into flour mixture; mix until dry ingredients are just moistened. Do not overmix. Gently fold in chopped mint candies.

Lightly grease 12 muffin cups or line with paper liners. Pour about ¹/₄ cup batter into each cup. Bake in a preheated 375-degree oven 15 to 18 minutes (it might be slightly longer if using paper liners), or until tops of muffins are slightly firm. (The "toothpick-inserted-in-the-center" test doesn't always work because of the melted chocolate in the center.) Let cool in pan about 5 minutes, then remove from pan and place on wire rack to cool completely.

*Note: My first attempt at mint muffins was both a failure and a success. I tried putting a mint chocolate drop on top of the plain chocolate batter in each cup and adding just a tablespoon of batter on top. The chocolate drop sank to the bottom like a depth charge and fused to the pan! This was pretty much a failure based on what I was trying to achieve. However, I think that if I used lightly greased foil liners, I would get Magic Mint Muffins to make with my nephews: "Watch while I make the chocolate drop disappear!" The mint drop would be the treat at the bottom of the cup. It's something to experiment with next time they come to visit.*

*If you have other kinds of chocolate mints on hand, use about 1 cup chopped pieces. The pieces should be about the size of regular chocolate morsels.*

# Fresh-Baked Breakfast

B reakfast is my favorite meal. Hands down, no contest, my refection of preference, the collation sensation, the only way to start the day. I have a weird, mystical, psychic link to waffles, to anything that requires maple syrup. In fact, at one time one of my life goals was to be able to pour just the right amount of syrup to make the pancakes and syrup come out even, which I have since achieved, on separate occasions, with pancakes, waffles and French toast.

But it's not just syrup that I crave. I like cold cereal, too, and Cream of Wheat and scrambled eggs and bacon and biscuits and sausage patties and hash browns and all those things on the buffet at nice hotels (one of the few genuine pleasures of media tours). I like cold milk and strong coffee and delicate teas and every kind of juice except prune, and I never met a fruit plate I didn't like. I'll eat yogurt, in a pinch, but would rather have a carrot muffin or cinnamon roll or even ordinary toast with butter and honey.

My passion for breakfast goes even further: it's my favorite meal to prepare for others. I'm always the first one up on camping trips because I love the smell of bacon frying in the open air. Back in my pre-monastery dating days, I would ask a girl to an autumn breakfast in the park: "I'll fix you breakfast and then we'll go walk through the leaves." If she didn't want to get up that early (or worse yet, just didn't like breakfast) I knew we would never last. But I knew the relationship might have some staying power if a girl thought breakfast in the park with a walk through the leaves sounded irresistibly romantic.

You'll find some irresistible recipes in this chapter, every one of them a perfect reason to get up early and treat someone you love to a freshly baked breakfast.

# FRENCH TOAST CUSTARD CASSEROLE

Yield: 1 serving.

2 thick or 3 medium slices **day-old bread**

1 **egg**

2 tablespoons **whole** or **reduced-fat milk**

2 tablespoons chopped **pecans**

$1/3$ cup **maple-flavored syrup**

1 tablespoon **butter**, cut into pieces

You will need an individual-serving-size ovenproof bowl, about 5 inches wide and 2 inches deep. Lightly grease bowl with vegetable cooking spray or butter.

Trim bread slices to a shape and size that will fit the ovenproof bowl. Combine egg and milk in a large bowl; whisk until well mixed. Put bread slices in egg mixture and let stand until liquid is absorbed.

Put pecans and maple syrup in ovenproof bowl. Dot with butter pieces. Place soaked bread slices on top; the bread should not reach past the lip of the bowl. Place bowl on a baking sheet to catch any drips. Bake in preheated 350-degree oven 30 to 35 minutes, or until top is lightly browned and center is firm. Let stand about 10 minutes, then invert bowl onto serving plate; remove bowl and serve.

*Note: This recipe produces a custard-like casserole, sort of like bread pudding with a maple-pecan sauce. If you like a drier French toast (as I do), actually cook the bread slices on a heated skillet as you normally would for regular French toast. Then reduce the amount of syrup to $1/4$ cup, assemble the casserole and bake as directed.*

*I don't recommend using ordinary supermarket sandwich bread for this recipe. Try Hungarian Potato Bread (page 113), a crunchy, textured bread like Nine-Grain Bread (page 20), or my favorite, Anadama Bread (page 32).*

## Bread Break

I have seen several recipes for large French toast casseroles, which usually make six to eight servings. But what if you're single—do you have to host a brunch before you get to try the recipe? Or what if you have the entire family for the holidays, but not everyone likes French toast? I developed these individual-serving casseroles so you can make as few or as many as you like. Just multiply the ingredient amounts as needed. At the abbey, we have a number of soup bowls with handles that are the perfect serving size. Look for them at any housewares store and make sure that they are ovenproof.

# Harvest Braid

Yield: 1 loaf.

## Bread Break

This braided beauty makes a dramatic centerpiece for an autumn family breakfast or an Easter brunch. The number of strips you cut is entirely up to you. Beginners might want to start with five wide strips, while more advanced bakers might cut them thinner. Either method makes an attractive loaf to adorn a buffet table.

1 recipe **Single Loaf White Bread dough** (page 28)

1 ½ cups coarsely chopped cooked **ham**

1 ½ cups shredded **sharp Cheddar cheese**

½ cup chopped **walnuts**

1 ¼ cups peeled and chopped **apple** (see note)

1 **egg white** beaten with 1 tablespoon **water**, for egg wash

Prepare dough for Single Loaf White Bread through the first rising. Punch down dough and knead briefly to expel large air bubbles. Roll out dough on lightly floured surface to a rectangle, 18x10 inches.

Prepare filling by combining ham, cheese, walnuts and apple in medium bowl; toss to mix. Spread filling lengthwise in the center third of the dough; press filling together slightly.

Using a sharp knife, cut each outer third of the dough (the part not covered by filling) into 5 to 10 diagonal strips, cutting from edge of dough to about 1 inch from edge of filling. Lightly brush strips with water. Fold strips over filling, alternating left and right, being careful not to stretch the dough. Tuck in ends of last strips; pinch to seal.

Carefully transfer loaf to a lightly greased 13x9x2-inch baking pan. Cover and let rise in a warm, draft-free place 30 minutes, or until doubled.

About 15 minutes before end of rising time, preheat oven to 400 degrees. Brush surface of loaf with egg wash. Bake loaf about 30 minutes, or until top is golden brown and temperature of the filling is about 160 degrees.

*Note:* *The apples I have used for this braid include Gala, Granny Smith, Lura Red and Northern Spy—all grown at our abbey orchard. Ask your grocer for advice if you're not sure which apples in your area are good for baking. Better still, visit a local orchard during harvest time and pick your own. You want a tart, crisp apple that will stand up to baking without turning to mush.*

*The apple adds a nice contrast to the salty ham and sharp cheese. Try other cheeses if you like. I have tried this recipe with blue cheese and white Cheddar, both with excellent results.*

# PUMPKIN PANCAKES

Yield: 12 to 16 pancakes.

1 ¼ cups **all-purpose flour**

1 tablespoon **baking powder**

1 tablespoon **granulated sugar**

½ teaspoon **salt**

½ teaspoon **ground cinnamon**

¼ teaspoon **ground nutmeg**

¼ teaspoon **ground ginger**

1 cup **milk**

2 **eggs**

1 cup canned **pumpkin puree**

¼ cup **oil**

Sift flour, baking powder, sugar, salt, cinnamon, nutmeg and ginger into medium bowl; stir until mixed. In another bowl, combine milk, eggs, pumpkin puree and oil; beat until well mixed. Add pumpkin mixture to flour mixture; stir until just mixed. Batter will be quite thick.

Preheat griddle according to manufacturer's instructions. For each pancake, spoon about ¼ cup batter onto griddle and flatten into a ¼-inch thick round. Cook over medium-high heat until bubbles form on the top, then turn and cook other side until browned. Serve immediately, or keep pancakes warm in oven until you have a platter full to serve.

*Note:* *The thickness of the batter might surprise you. It doesn't pour at all, but if you add more liquid, the pumpkin flavor becomes diluted.*

## Bread Break

Bob and Marilyn Haslam are members of the herb guild to which I belong. They run a charming bed-and-breakfast inn called Yesterday's Memories in nearby Princeton, Illinois. They used to serve these pumpkin pancakes only in the fall, but their guests began to ask for them all year 'round, so now they are a regular feature on the B&B menu. Marilyn serves these hotcakes with cooked apples and maple pecan syrup.

# FABS' NUTTY GOODNESS ROLLS

Yield: 12 rolls.

## Bread Break

I cannot make these rolls often enough for my students. Once when I was mixing the filling, one of the alumni, Jason "Fabs" Fabish, looked at the bowl of sugar, butter and nuts for the filling and exclaimed in a whisper, "Ohhhhhhhh—nutty goodness!" We have called them Fabs' Nutty Goodness Rolls ever since.

Fabs wants to become a professional bowler, and the discount store where he works once held a bake sale to raise money for his tournament fees. Naturally I promised him Nutty Goodness Rolls to sell. I made them in individual servings, using Texas-size muffin tins. I divided the caramel and nuts into each of the tins, then put one sliced roll in each. They turned out beautifully and sold out in a matter of minutes! If you make Nutty Goodness Rolls for your bake sale, don't be afraid to charge premium prices—ours were priced at $2 apiece, but $2.50 would not be too much to ask.

2 packages **FLEISCHMANN'S Active Dry Yeast**

$1/2$ cup lukewarm **water**

1 $1/2$ cups **sour cream**

2 tablespoons **vegetable oil**

### DOUGH:

$1/2$ cup **granulated sugar**

$1/4$ teaspoon **baking soda**

2 teaspoons **salt**

2 **eggs**

4 $1/2$ cups **all-purpose flour**

### FILLING:

$1/3$ cup packed **brown sugar**

$1/3$ cup **granulated sugar**

$1/4$ cup **all-purpose flour**

1 tablespoon **ground cinnamon**

$1/4$ cup ($1/2$ stick) **butter**, cold, cut into $1/2$-inch slices

$1/2$ cup chopped **pecans**

### NUTTY GOODNESS CARAMEL SAUCE:

$1/2$ cup (1 stick) **butter**

1 cup packed **brown sugar**

$1/4$ cup **light corn syrup**

$3/4$ cup chopped **pecans**

Sprinkle yeast over lukewarm water in a small bowl; stir to dissolve. Let stand 10 minutes, or until foamy.

Combine sour cream, oil and sugar in saucepan; place over medium heat, stirring occasionally, until sugar is completely dissolved and the mixture is smooth. Do not boil. Remove from heat and stir in baking soda and salt. Let cool to lukewarm.

Pour sour cream mixture into large bowl. Add yeast mixture and eggs; stir until smooth. Add flour, about 1 cup at a time, mixing well after each addition. Turn out dough onto lightly floured surface; knead about 3 minutes. Dough will be quite sticky, but avoid the temptation to add too much more flour—just a tablespoon or two to keep the dough manageable. Let dough rest about 10 minutes; it will firm up nicely during this time.

Meanwhile, prepare filling: Combine brown sugar, granulated

sugar, flour and cinnamon in small bowl; stir to mix. Sprinkle cold butter pieces on top. Cut butter into sugar mixture with a pastry blender or two knives until mixture resembles coarse crumbs. Stir in pecans. Set filling aside.

Prepare caramel sauce: Combine butter, brown sugar and corn syrup in small saucepan. Cook over medium heat, stirring frequently, just until butter is melted and sugar is dissolved. Remove from heat and let cool slightly. Pour caramel sauce into a lightly greased 13x9x2-inch baking pan; sprinkle pecans on top of sauce. Set pan aside.

Roll out dough on lightly floured surface into a rectangle, 18x16 inches. Sprinkle filling over dough. Roll up dough from long side, jelly-roll style; pinch edge to seal (brush edge with a little water if necessary to make it stick). Cut roll crosswise into 12 pieces. Place pieces, cut-side down, on caramel sauce in pan. Cover and let rise 45 to 60 minutes, or until nearly doubled.

About 15 minutes before end of rising time, preheat oven to 375 degrees. Place baking pan on a jelly-roll pan or baking sheet to catch any drips. Bake 30 to 35 minutes, or until done. Invert onto serving plate while still warm.

〜

**Note:** *When you first mix the dough, it will seem much too moist and sticky, but the 10-minute rest really does make it firm up. If the weather is extremely humid and your kitchen isn't air-conditioned, you might add up to another $1/2$ cup flour during mixing, but no more.*

Bread Machine

# FABS' NUTTY GOODNESS ROLLS

Yield: 9 rolls.

### DOUGH:

$^1/_4$ cup **water**

$^3/_4$ cup **sour cream**

1 tablespoon **vegetable oil**

1 **egg**

1 teaspoon **salt**

2 $^1/_4$ cups plus 2 tablespoons **bread flour**

$^1/_8$ teaspoon **baking soda**

$^1/_4$ cup **granulated sugar**

1 $^1/_2$ teaspoons **FLEISCHMANN'S** Bread Machine Yeast

### FILLING:

2 $^1/_2$ tablespoons **brown sugar**

2 $^1/_2$ tablespoons **granulated sugar**

2 tablespoons **all-purpose flour**

1 $^1/_2$ teaspoons **ground cinnamon**

2 tablespoons **butter**, cut into pieces

$^1/_4$ cup chopped **pecans**

### NUTTY GOODNESS CARAMEL SAUCE:

$^1/_4$ cup ($^1/_2$ stick) **butter**

$^1/_2$ cup packed **brown sugar**

2 tablespoons **light corn syrup**

$^1/_3$ cup chopped **pecans**

Add water, sour cream, oil, egg, salt, bread flour, baking soda, sugar and yeast to bread machine pan in the order suggested by manufacturer. Select **dough/manual cycle.**

Meanwhile, prepare filling: Combine brown sugar, granulated sugar, flour and cinnamon in medium bowl; stir to mix. Sprinkle butter pieces on top. With pastry blender or two knives, cut butter into sugar mixture until mixture resembles coarse crumbs. Stir in pecans. Set filling aside.

Prepare caramel sauce: Combine butter, brown sugar and corn syrup in small saucepan. Cook over medium heat, stirring frequently, until sugar is dissolved. Remove from heat and let cool slightly. Pour caramel sauce into lightly greased 8 x 8-inch square baking pan. Sprinkle pecans on sauce. Set pan aside.

When cycle is complete, remove dough from machine to

floured surface. Roll out dough to 16x10-inch rectangle. Sprinkle filling over dough. Beginning at long end, roll up tightly as for jelly roll. Pinch seam to seal. Cut into 9 equal pieces. Place pieces, cut-side down, on caramel sauce in pan. Cover and let rise in a warm, draft-free place about 45 minutes, or until doubled.

Bake in a preheated 375-degree oven 30 to 35 minutes, or until done. Invert onto serving plate while still warm.

Yield: 2 flower loaves.

## Bread Break

This recipe is NOT for Mom to make for herself, but for Dad, kids, grandchildren, babysitters, etc. to make for Mom. Mom shouldn't have to make her own present, or clean up the kitchen afterward. The recipe uses fast-rising yeast, so small children won't lose interest during a long first-rising period. During the brief 10-minute rest, you can have them help clean up the kitchen, and during the longer rise before baking, they can make the appropriate decorations for the flower. Children can cut large leaves out of green construction paper, write messages on them and use them to decorate the serving platter. A child's school picture might be glued to a construction paper butterfly; tape the butterfly to a wooden pick and insert it in the center of the flower.

Some viewers may wonder if a celibate monk has any business creating recipes for kids in the kitchen. But have no fear—this recipe was

3 ¹/₄ to 3 ¹/₂ cups **all-purpose flour**, divided

1 package **FLEISCHMANN'S RapidRise Yeast**

1 teaspoon **salt**

1 cup **milk**

1 tablespoon **vegetable oil**

2 tablespoons **granulated sugar**

1 **egg**, beaten

1 teaspoon **vanilla extract**

1 cup **Mom's choice** (nuts, dried fruit, chocolate, etc.; see note)

**For decoration:** colored frosting, candy sprinkles, etc. (optional)

Sift 2 cups of the flour, yeast and salt into a medium bowl; stir until well mixed. Combine milk, oil and sugar in a small saucepan; heat to 120 to 130 degrees. Pour milk mixture into flour mixture; beat well. Add egg and vanilla; stir until well mixed. Add 1 cup of the remaining flour; stir until flour is thoroughly incorporated. Gradually add enough of the remaining flour to make a soft dough that is rather sticky.

Turn out dough onto a lightly floured surface. Knead 3 minutes, or until dough has a consistent texture. Cover with a slightly damp cloth and let rest 10 minutes. Flatten dough into a rough oval. Scatter the 1 cup Mom's choice (nuts, dried fruit, etc.) in center of dough. Fold up sides of dough. Knead until nuts (or dried fruit, chocolate, etc.) are evenly distributed.

Divide dough in half; divide each half into 6 equal pieces, for a total of 12 pieces. Roll 5 pieces into short, fat ropes, about 8 inches long. Form each rope into a horseshoe shape; arrange like the petals of a flower (see illustration) on one side of a lightly greased baking sheet. Roll one piece of dough into a ball; place ball in center of flower and flatten slightly. Repeat with remaining 6 pieces of dough to make a second flower. Cover and let rise in a warm, draft-free place about 1 hour, or until doubled.

About 15 minutes before end of rising time, preheat oven to 350 degrees. Place on middle rack of oven and bake 15 to 20 minutes, or until top is brown. Carefully remove flower loaves from baking sheet and let cool completely on wire rack.

If desired, frost petals and center of flower, and decorate with sprinkles.

**Note:** *The "Mom's choice" in the ingredient list refers to whatever goodies Mom likes best: raisins or dried cranberries, chocolate morsels, walnuts, toffee chunks, etc. For my own mother, I'd use dried blueberries and chopped pecans and serve the flower with Irish Breakfast tea. The pieces should be no larger than a raisin or chocolate morsel, or they will interfere with the shaping of the flower.*

kid-tested by the daughter of my kitchen angel Bridget. Five-year-old Taylor helped me form and frost the flower, and prepared the construction paper leaves that were used on camera.

Bread Machine

# MOTHER'S DAY FLOWERS

Yield: 2 flowers.

¹/₂ cup **water**

¹/₂ cup **milk**

1 **egg**

1 tablespoon **vegetable oil**

1 teaspoon **vanilla extract**

1 teaspoon **salt**

3 cups **bread flour**

2 tablespoons **granulated sugar**

2 teaspoons
· **FLEISCHMANN'S Bread Machine Yeast**

1 cup **Mom's choice** (nuts, dried fruits, chocolate, etc.)

**For decoration:** colored frosting, candy sprinkles, etc. (optional)

Add water, milk, egg, oil, vanilla, salt, bread flour, sugar, yeast and Mom's Choice (1 cup nuts, dried fruits, etc.) to bread machine pan in the order recommended by manufacturer. Select **dough/manual cycle**.

When cycle is complete, remove dough from bread machine. Divide dough in half; divide each half into 6 equal pieces, for a total of 12 pieces. Roll 5 pieces into short, fat ropes, about 8 inches long. Form each rope into a horseshoe shape; arrange like the petals of a flower on one side of a greased baking sheet. Roll one piece of dough into a ball; place ball in center of flower and flatten slightly. Repeat with remaining 6 pieces of dough to make second flower. Cover and let rise in a warm, draft-free place about 1 hour, or until doubled.

Bake in a preheated 350-degree oven 15 minutes, or until done. Carefully remove flowers from baking sheet and place on wire rack to cool completely.

If desired, frost petals and center of flower, and decorate with sprinkles.

# POPOVERS

Yield: 6 popovers.

| | |
|---|---|
| 1 cup **all-purpose flour** | 2 **eggs** |
| ¹/₂ teaspoon **salt** | 1 tablespoon **butter**, melted |
| 1 cup **milk** or **buttermilk** | 6 small pieces **butter** (about ¹/₂ teaspoon each) |

Bring all ingredients to room temperature. Preheat oven to 425 degrees.

Combine flour and salt in 1-quart bowl; stir to mix. Combine milk, eggs and melted butter in another bowl; mix well. Gradually pour egg mixture into flour mixture, stirring constantly. Beat until smooth (I like to use a small whisk).

Place one small piece butter in bottom of each section of popover pan. Place pan in preheated oven about 1 minute, or until butter is bubbling. Remove pan from oven. Divide batter among the six sections of the pan (about ²/₃ cup in each). Bake in 425-degree oven 20 minutes (don't open the oven to peek or the popovers will fall), then reduce oven temperature to 325 degrees and bake 10 minutes. Remove from oven and prick the top of each popover with a fork a couple of times. Return to oven and bake 5 minutes. The popovers will be golden brown and rather firm on top. Remove from oven and let cool in pan about 10 minutes before removing popovers. Serve warm with butter and honey, if desired.

*Note: Popovers are versatile breads and are delicious in any number of ways. Of my three studio interns, Keith slathers his with butter and honey, David prefers his with grape jelly, and Chris cuts off the top and fills the popover with chocolate pudding. Popovers can be served hot filled with shrimp in garlic cream sauce, or cold with herbed cheese spread.*

## Bread Break

I first learned about popovers from a delightful Irish lady named Kate, who was working as the house-keeper at a parish where I was substituting one week-end. She served me fresh popovers at supper, and I became an instant fan. I asked her for her secret, and she confided in a near whisper, "You have to bring the ingredients to room temperature before you mix a thing, or they just won't pop." She wrote down her exact recipe for me (which I have since lost, to my regret), but her advice remains with me as the key to perfect popovers.

# PUMPKIN BUBBLE SPICE RING

Yield: 1 ring; about 12 servings.

## Bread Break

A few years ago I had a piece of pumpkin pie with a layer of cream cheese filling on the bottom. I found the combination of flavors and textures quite tasty. I was inspired to experiment with similar ingredients for this pull-apart bread. The cream cheese is an unexpected surprise for some. When I first served this to the community, Father Patrick bit into a piece and thought, "Oh no, it's not baked all the way through!" Once he realized that the white center was cream cheese and not unbaked dough, he had a couple more pieces.

2 ¹/₂ cups **all-purpose flour**, divided

¹/₃ cup **granulated sugar**

1 teaspoon **salt**

1 ¹/₂ teaspoons **ground cinnamon**

¹/₄ teaspoon **ground nutmeg**

1 package **FLEISCHMANN'S RapidRise Yeast**

³/₄ cup canned **pumpkin puree**

¹/₄ cup **milk**

1 **egg**, beaten

¹/₄ cup **light corn syrup**

¹/₂ cup packed **brown sugar**

¹/₄ cup (¹/₂ stick) **butter**

1 cup finely chopped **pecans** or **walnuts**, divided

2 (3-ounce) packages **cream cheese**

Combine 1 cup of the flour, granulated sugar, salt, cinnamon, nutmeg and yeast in medium bowl; stir until well mixed. Combine pumpkin puree and milk in small saucepan; heat to 120 to 130 degrees. Pour pumpkin mixture into flour mixture; stir until well blended. Add egg; mix well. Add 1 cup of the flour; stir until flour is thoroughly incorporated. Add enough of the remaining flour, about ¹/₄ cup at a time, to make a rather soft dough.

Turn out dough onto lightly floured surface. Knead 5 minutes. Cover dough with a damp cloth and let rest 10 minutes.

Meanwhile, combine corn syrup, brown sugar and butter in small saucepan. Cook over medium heat, stirring constantly, until butter is melted and sugar is completely dissolved. Remove from heat. Lightly grease a 10-inch fluted tube or Bundt pan. Sprinkle half of the nuts in bottom of pan; pour in half of the caramel mixture.

Cut cream cheese into 20 pieces and roll each piece into a ball. Knead dough one minute, then divide dough into 20 pieces. Flatten each piece of dough and wrap it around a piece of cream cheese. Arrange 10 pieces of cream cheese-filled dough in a single layer in the pan. Sprinkle the remaining nuts on top. Arrange remaining 10 pieces of cream cheese-filled dough on top of first layer. Pour remaining caramel mixture over all. Cover with plastic wrap and let rise in a warm, draft-free place about 1 hour, or until doubled. The risen dough will not quite reach the top of the pan.

About 15 minutes before end of rising time, preheat oven to 350 degrees. Bake 25 to 30 minutes, or until lightly browned on top. Let cool in pan 10 minutes, then invert onto a serving platter. Can be served warm or cool.

*Note: The dough itself isn't very sweet, because I think the caramel sauce has enough sugar. You could make a nicely sweet pumpkin bread by increasing the sugar to $^1/_2$ cup and simply forming the dough into a loaf for a lightly greased $8^1/_2$ x $4^1/_2$ x $2^1/_2$-inch loaf pan. The baking time would be about the same.*

*The real question is, "What do I do with the leftover pumpkin puree besides let it go bad in the fridge?" For the answer to that query, see the recipe for Pumpkin Pancakes (page 55), which can be mixed and baked while the Pumpkin Bubble Spice Ring is rising.*

Bread Machine

# PUMPKIN BUBBLE SPICE RING

Yield: 1 ring.

$^1/_4$ cup **milk**

2 tablespoons **water**

1 **egg**

$^3/_4$ cup canned **pumpkin puree**

1 teaspoon **salt**

2 $^1/_2$ cups **bread flour**

$^1/_3$ cup **granulated sugar**

1 $^1/_2$ teaspoons **ground cinnamon**

$^1/_4$ teaspoon **ground nutmeg**

2 teaspoons **FLEISCHMANN'S Bread Machine Yeast**

$^1/_2$ cup packed **brown sugar**

$^1/_4$ cup **light corn syrup**

$^1/_4$ cup ($^1/_2$ stick) **butter** or **margarine**

2 (3-ounce) packages **cream cheese**, cut into 20 pieces and rolled into balls

1 cup finely chopped **pecans** or **walnuts**, divided

Add milk, water, egg, pumpkin puree, salt, bread flour, sugar, cinnamon, nutmeg and yeast to bread machine pan in the order suggested by manufacturer. Select **dough/manual cycle**.

Meanwhile, combine brown sugar, corn syrup and butter in small saucepan. Cook over medium heat, stirring constantly, until butter is melted and sugar is completely dissolved. Remove from heat.

When cycle is complete, remove dough from machine. Cover and let rest 10 minutes. Divide dough into 20 equal pieces. Flatten each piece and wrap it around a cream cheese ball. Sprinkle half the nuts in bottom of greased 10-inch fluted tube or Bundt pan. Pour half the caramel mixture over nuts. Arrange 10 cream cheese-filled dough balls in a single layer in the pan; sprinkle with remaining nuts. Arrange remaining filled balls on top of first layer. Pour remaining caramel mixture over all. Cover and let rise in a warm, draft-free place about 1 hour, or until doubled.

Bake in a preheated 350-degree oven 20 to 25 minutes, or until lightly browned. Let cool 10 minutes in pan on wire rack. Invert onto serving platter. Serve warm or cool.

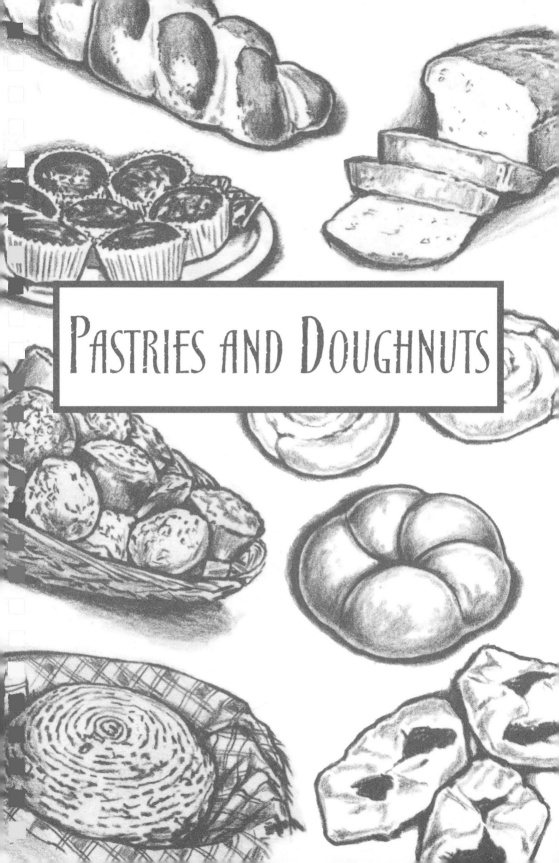

# Pastries and Doughnuts

For many years, one of my culinary life goals was to learn to make Danish pastry, and in my exploration of pastry, I have made a number of discoveries:

The two most important tools you need for pastry making are patience and a rolling pin. Pastry dough has to be refrigerated between rollings, and it does take a little bit of time. But if you've heard that making pastry is unbearably hard, I beg to differ. If you can roll out dough into a roughly rectangular shape to make cinnamon rolls, you can make pastry.

Beating a pound of butter with a rolling pin is the best part of pastry making. I read several recipes that started with a thick slab of butter between layers of dough. But if you roll the butter out into a thin, flexible sheet first (this requires several minutes of unrestrained, exuberant beating), it's a whole lot easier to achieve the multiple layers that make flaky pastry. Read the instructions on page 69, and you'll see what I mean.

When it comes to forming pastries, smaller is better. I don't know who decided that a prune Danish had to be the size of a baseball glove, but he should be banned from the kitchen. Smaller pastries are better, because they bake faster, are easier to handle and eat, and you don't feel guilty for having eaten one or two.

Smaller pastries mean there are more to share. During taping we sometimes produced nearly a hundred pastries in a day. So my student interns and I decided to treat the firemen at St. Louis Fire Station #21, which we passed every day on our way to and from the station. They proved to be so appreciative that we made it a regular practice, and during the three weeks of taping we dropped off almond bear claws, croissants, herb bread, cinnamon rolls—whatever had been baked that day and looked good enough to give away. You might consider doing the same for the firemen, police and EMTs who serve your neighborhood. With the recipes that follow, you'll have plenty to share.

# DANISH PASTRY DOUGH

Yield: Enough dough for 32 to 40 pastries.

2 packages **FLEISCHMANN'S Active Dry Yeast**

$^1/_2$ cup lukewarm **water**

Pinch **granulated sugar**

$^1/_3$ cup **granulated sugar**

$^3/_4$ cup **milk**, cold

2 **eggs**

1 teaspoon **salt**

4 $^1/_2$ cups **all-purpose** or **pastry flour**, divided

1 pound (4 sticks) **butter**, cold

Sprinkle yeast over lukewarm water in large bowl; add a pinch of sugar. Stir to dissolve yeast. Let stand about 10 minutes, or until foamy.

Add $^1/_3$ cup sugar, milk, eggs and salt to yeast mixture; stir until blended. Add 3 cups of the flour; beat about 2 minutes, or until smooth. Gradually add the remaining 1 $^1/_2$ cups flour, stirring until flour is thoroughly incorporated, but don't overwork the dough. The mixture will be halfway between batter and bread dough; your bread baking instincts will be screaming at you to add more flour, but turn a deaf ear. Cover the bowl with plastic wrap and refrigerate at least 60 minutes.

Place the cold butter on a large piece of waxed paper or parchment paper. Knead butter about 5 minutes to make it more pliable (it will be brittle at first, but persevere). Form butter into a flattened rectangle. Place rectangle between two large pieces of waxed paper. Roll out butter into a rectangle about 16x10 inches. Leave butter between waxed paper and refrigerate it until firm.

Remove dough from refrigerator. Set aside a piece of dough about the size of a small walnut; this is your emergency repair kit, which you will need if you are a beginner like me. Place dough on a well-floured surface or pastry cloth; roll out dough into a rectangle about 24x18 inches. Peel the top layer of waxed paper off the butter, and turn it over onto one half of the dough.

## Bread Break

This recipe is based on one I got from my fellow gardener Judy, who belongs to the same herb guild as I do. Her directions were much more concise than mine; they were handwritten on a single 3x5-inch card! I thought it would be best to expand a bit for beginners. Don't let the seeming complexity of the directions keep you from trying. If you can roll out pizza dough into a circle, you can make Danish pastry. The first time I tried it, it was so easy that I berated myself for not trying it years ago.

Peel off the remaining waxed paper. Brush the edges of the dough with water. Fold the dough on one side over the butter and dough of the other side, stretching dough gently to line up the edges as needed. Press edges to seal. You now have an envelope of dough, 18x12 inches, with a butter love letter tucked inside.

Fold one-third of dough over center of dough, and the remaining third over that, to make a triple-decker package, 12x6 inches. Line up the edges carefully and press them together. Turn the dough so the 6-inch side is directly in front  of you. Very lightly dust the top with flour. Roll out dough into a rectangle, 18x12 inches. Fold dough again into a triple-decker package; wrap in waxed paper and refrigerate 15 minutes. (You now have 27 layers of butter in the dough.)

Repeat this process—roll out, fold, refrigerate—two more times, after which you will have 27 x 3 x 3 = 243 layers of butter in the dough. If in the process of kneading, a hole appears in the dough and the butter sticks out, cover it with a small piece of your emergency repair kit.

Refrigerate the dough for a final 30 minutes, or overnight. It will then be ready to form into Danish pastries (see recipes). If you refrigerate it overnight, be sure to wrap it loosely but thoroughly; I wrap mine once loosely in waxed paper, then once in plastic wrap. The dough will expand in the fridge, and you don't want it to blow out of the wrapper.

≈

*Note: Don't attempt Danish pastry in a hot kitchen in July unless you are a real whiz with a rolling pin and can work quickly. The butter has to be cold in order to remain as a distinct layer from the dough. All those layers are what make the pastries light. The water in the dough turns to steam in the hot oven and forces the layers apart, and once the butter heats up, it essentially french fries each layer of dough.*

# ALMOND BEAR CLAW PASTRIES

Yield: 40 small pastries.

1 recipe **Danish Pastry Dough** (page 69)

1 (12-ounce) can **almond filling**

¹/₂ cup **light corn syrup**

Divide dough in half; wrap one half in plastic wrap and refrigerate. Place other half of dough on a well-floured surface or pastry cloth. Roll dough into a rectangle about 18x12 inches. Trim rectangle to 16x10 inches; reserve pastry scraps for other uses (such as samples for the baker). Cut rectangle into 4x2-inch pieces. Spread 1 teaspoon almond filling down center of each piece. Brush edges of each piece with water, fold dough over filling and press to seal. Bend each piece into a semicircle; the seam should be on the inner (narrow) curve. Place on ungreased baking sheet or jelly-roll pan. With sharp kitchen scissors, make four evenly spaced cuts on the wide curve of each bear claw; be careful not to cut too deep or the filling will leak out during baking.

Repeat process with second half of dough and remaining almond filling.

Let bear claws rise in a warm, draft-free place 30 to 45 minutes, or until doubled. About 15 minutes before end of rising time, preheat oven to 350 degrees. Bake bear claws 15 to 20 minutes, or until golden brown and slightly firm to the touch. Remove from pan and transfer to wire rack.

Heat corn syrup in microwave oven on High (100 percent) power 45 seconds. Use a soft pastry brush to brush hot corn syrup on still-hot bear claws. Let cool slightly on wire racks and serve warm.

## Bread Break

The first time my buddy Keith tried one of these bear claws warm from the oven, he quipped, "I didn't know that you knew Satan and exchanged recipes with him. These are sinful!" I prefer to think of them as a little bit of heaven.

These little almond pastries are definitely not for everyday. They're a lot of work and very high in fat, but for special occasions they are worth the effort.

Even though these are small, 40 pastries is a lot. If you double-wrap the second half of dough (once in waxed paper, once in plastic wrap), you can freeze it for up to a month. For my large family of monks, I use half the dough for bear claws, the other half for Cinnamon Pastry Spirals (page 72). Whatever might be left from the monks' breakfast is eaten by the crew from the St. Bede Abbey Press during their morning coffee break.

# Cinnamon Pastry Spirals

Yield: About 32 small pastries.

## Bread Break

On a breakfast buffet table, these cinnamon-sugar delights are a nice surprise. Your guests expect an ordinary cinnamon roll, but get one of these incredibly light and buttery pastries instead. Resist the temptation to add more frosting or glaze, and place them far away from the butter dish—these are perfect just as they are.

Unless you have a large family, it's unlikely that you'll need 32 pastries at breakfast. Prepare a plate for a neighbor, take a dozen to the office or just pass them out to anyone who comes to the door.

1 recipe **Danish Pastry Dough** (page 69)

1 cup **granulated sugar**

4 teaspoons **ground cinnamon**

$^1/_2$ cup **light corn syrup**

Divide dough in half; wrap one half in plastic wrap and refrigerate. Place other half of dough on a well-floured surface or pastry cloth. Roll dough into a rectangle about 16x12 inches. Combine sugar and cinnamon in a small bowl; stir to mix. Sprinkle dough with half of the cinnamon-sugar. Starting with the long edge, roll up dough, jelly-roll style. Brush edge with water and pinch to seal. Cut roll into 1-inch rounds. Place rounds, cut-side down, on ungreased baking sheet or jelly-roll pan.

Repeat process with second half of dough and remaining cinnamon-sugar.

Let spirals rise in a warm, draft-free place 30 to 45 minutes, or until doubled. About 15 minutes before end of rising time, preheat oven to 350 degrees. Bake spirals 15 to 20 minutes, or until golden brown and slightly firm to the touch. Remove from pan and transfer to wire rack.

Heat corn syrup in microwave on High (100 percent) power 45 seconds. Use a soft pastry brush to brush hot corn syrup on still-hot spirals. Let cool slightly on wire racks and serve warm.

*Note: If you like a slightly crisper crust on your pastry, you can bake these 5 minutes longer, but be careful not to let the bottoms burn.*

# BASIC BATTER DOUGHNUTS

Yield: 14 to 18 doughnuts.

2 ¹/₄ cups **all-purpose flour**

³/₄ cup **granulated sugar**

2 teaspoons **baking powder**

1 teaspoon **salt**

¹/₄ teaspoon freshly grated **nutmeg**

2 **eggs**

1 cup **milk** (see note)

1 tablespoon **vegetable oil**

1 teaspoon **vanilla extract**

Sift flour, sugar, baking powder, salt and nutmeg into a medium bowl; stir until well mixed. In another bowl, whisk together eggs, milk, oil and vanilla. Pour egg mixture into flour mixture; beat until smooth.

Pour batter into doughnut maker or doughnut pans and bake according to manufacturer's instructions. Or, use a doughnut batter dispenser (see note) and fry the doughnuts in 2 inches of oil heated to 365 to 375 degrees, about 2 minutes per side.

❧

*Note: This recipe works well with the nonstick doughnut pans you see in cookware stores and catalogs. Although such pans do produce a low-fat doughnut, I find the doughnuts don't brown very well, so I'm not a big fan. However, when I put these doughnuts, sprinkled with confectioners' sugar, on the breakfast table at the abbey, they are always eaten.*

*If you use a doughnut batter dispenser (such as the old red and white Popeil Brothers, or a Mirro cookie press with the doughnut attachment), reduce the amount of milk to ³/₄ cup for a thicker batter. A thinner batter comes out too quickly and makes a misshapen doughnut.*

## Bread Break

As regular viewers of the program know, I have a great fondness for rummage sales, secondhand shops and antique malls. I find kitchen gadgets almost irresistible, although I must say that I don't buy them unless I know I can use them. If they are too fragile to be used or serve some purpose outside my usual kitchen activities, I leave them for someone else. But when I saw an old-fashioned red-and-white plastic batter doughnut press, still in its original box, at our Academy's semi-annual rummage sale, I knew I had to give it a good home. I was even more delighted with my find when I discovered a hand-written recipe card, much stained with use, tucked in the bottom of the box—the recipe here is based on it.

# SHORTCUT CROISSANTS

Yield: 28 small croissants.

## Bread Break

Despite the long directions, this recipe really is a time-saver compared to making full-blown pastry, because the butter is cut into the flour and you don't need to chill the dough every time you roll it out. These are not quite as flaky as genuine croissants, but far better than ordinary crescent rolls.

These little rolls are meant to be served at breakfast with honey, or at tea with homemade apricot preserves, but NOT as a base for sandwiches. If you are going to the trouble to bake homemade croissants, don't spoil them by covering their delicate flavors with spicy lunch meats. And after all the effort to make your rolls puff up, why squish them flat as a sandwich?

3 ¹/₂ cups **all-purpose flour**, divided

1 cup (2 sticks) **butter**, cold, cut into ¹/₂-inch slices

1 package **FLEISCHMANN'S RapidRise Yeast**

2 tablespoons **granulated sugar**

¹/₂ teaspoon **salt**

1 cup **milk**

1 **egg**, lightly beaten

Additional **flour**, for dusting

1 **egg** beaten with 2 tablespoons warm **water**, for egg wash (optional)

Put 1¹/₂ cups of the flour in a medium bowl. Add cold butter slices and toss to coat. Briefly cut butter into flour using a pastry blender or two knives, until butter pieces are about the size of lima beans (larger than for pie crust). Refrigerate butter mixture while you proceed with recipe.

Combine yeast, sugar, salt and remaining 2 cups flour in medium bowl; stir until well mixed. Put milk in small saucepan and heat to 120 to 130 degrees. Pour milk into flour mixture; beat until smooth. Stir in egg; beat by hand 2 or 3 minutes. Let batter rest 15 minutes.

Stir down batter. Remove butter mixture from refrigerator and add to batter. Stir until well mixed. Cover bowl with plastic wrap and refrigerate at least 2 hours.

Turn out dough onto a well-floured surface or pastry cloth. Roll out dough into an 18x12-inch rectangle. The dough will be lumpy because of the butter pieces. Fold one-third of dough over center of dough, and the remaining one-third over that, making a triple-decker package, about 12x6 inches. Line up edges carefully and press them together. Turn dough so the 6-inch side is directly in front of you; lightly dust top with flour. Again, roll out dough to 18x12-inch rectangle. Fold again into a triple-decker and turn again. Repeat this process—roll out, fold, turn—three more times, keeping the work surface and the dough well dusted with flour as you work. Wrap dough loosely in parchment paper or waxed paper, then in plastic wrap; refrigerate at least one hour, or overnight.

Divide dough into 2 equal pieces. On a well-floured surface or pastry cloth, roll out one piece of dough into 13x13-inch square. Trim dough to 12x12 inches. Using a pizza cutter or sharp knife, cut dough into two rectangles. Cut out elongated triangles according to diagram. Starting from the 3-inch side, roll each triangle loosely toward the point. Place point-side down on ungreased baking sheet and curve ends to form croissant. Repeat with remaining piece of dough; use a second baking sheet if needed. (The trimmings can be tied into loose knots and baked, to enjoy as baker's samples.) Cover with a light cloth and let rise in a warm, draft-free place 45 to 60 minutes, or until doubled.

About 15 minutes before end of rising time, preheat oven to 400 degrees. If desired, brush risen croissants with egg wash. Bake 10 minutes, or until golden brown. Remove from baking sheets and let cool on wire racks.

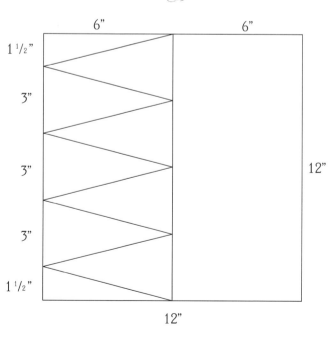

# SOUR CREAM DOUGHNUTS

Yield: 20 to 24 (3-inch) doughnuts, plus doughnut holes.

## Bread Break

The best old-fashioned sour cream doughnuts in my experience were served at the Mister Donut on Knoxville in Peoria, Illinois. I spent many a late night there with a group of friends or a date as the last stop before curfew. There was a large window into the kitchen where you could watch them make the doughnuts. One of the bakers would cut out doughnuts and flick the cutter so the doughnut would fly onto the thumb of his free hand, which made the hole pop out. In a matter of seconds, he'd gather three or four by this method, then line them up on the wire rack for frying. You could watch him fill a rack of four dozen in just a few minutes.

3 ³/₄ cups **all-purpose flour**

¹/₃ cup **granulated sugar**

1 ¹/₂ teaspoons **baking powder**

¹/₂ teaspoon **salt**

¹/₄ teaspoon **baking soda**

1 ¹/₂ cups **sour cream**

1 **egg**

**Vegetable oil**, for frying

**Confectioners' sugar**, for sprinkling

Sift flour, sugar, baking powder, salt and baking soda into medium bowl; stir to mix. In another bowl, combine sour cream and egg; mix well. Pour sour cream mixture into flour mixture; stir until just moistened. Turn out dough onto a lightly floured surface. Knead about 8 strokes, just enough make a cohesive dough. Let dough rest 10 minutes.

On a lightly floured surface, roll out dough to a thickness of about ¹/₂ inch. Cut out doughnuts using a 3- or 4-inch doughnut cutter. Press dough scraps together gently (do not knead), roll out, and cut more doughnuts. (Do not roll a third time; just fry the scraps as oddly shaped doughnut holes.) Let doughnuts firm up, uncovered, about 30 minutes. (I usually cut mine out and place them on a lightly greased baking sheet.)

Pour oil to a depth of 2 ¹/₂ to 3 inches in an electric fryer or skillet. (I recommend using an electric fryer with a calibrated dial, but you can use a deep skillet on the stovetop if you have a candy thermometer.) Heat oil to 365 to 375 degrees. Fry doughnuts, 3 or 4 at a time, about 2 minutes per side, or until medium brown. Drain on paper towels. Sprinkle confectioners' sugar on one side; serve warm. Recommended beverage: ice-cold chocolate milk.

*Note: Recipes for sour cream doughnuts vary greatly regarding the proportion of eggs and sour cream to flour and sugar. I've taken the middle road here, so these aren't as rich as some doughnuts and defi-*

*nitely require a sprinkling of confectioners' sugar to be their best. You can use cinnamon-sugar, too. I've also served them with a simple milk-and-confectioners'-sugar frosting, which my fellow monks seemed to enjoy very much. I'm assuming this based on the fact that there weren't any doughnuts left by the time I got to breakfast!*

*You might have seen me make doughnuts and samosas in a skillet on the program. I have switched to an electric fryer because it's easier to get precise temperature control (it took me nearly an hour to get that right in season one!). Also, the fryer on the countertop is more stable than a pan on the stove, and therefore safer in my view.*

*As with biscuits, it really is crucial to handle the dough as little as possible, or else the doughnuts will be tough rather than light and tender.*

# Savory Flavors

My Grandma Tootsie was full-blood Irish, having been the American-born product of the Cassidy, Cahill, Guile and McNulty clans from County Mayo, God help us. Her grandfather was a Cassidy who lived on a farm in Iowa with his five lovely daughters. At ice cream socials and barn dances, Mr. Cassidy would pull up in the buckboard wagon with his girls, which prompted the local saying, "The Cassidys have come, the party's begun!" Grandma inherited their love for hilarity and sociability, which she passed on to my mother and to all of us grandchildren.

Grandma Tootsie also had a real flair for storytelling and expressed herself well in speaking and writing. My whole family is blessed with a love for language and the ability to use it well. My sister Angela is writing a collection of family stories, my brother Marty is a librarian, as is my sister Eileen (her alliterative birthday messages are legendary in the family), and recently my brother Vincent e-mailed us a reflection on fatherhood that brought tears to our eyes. My grandmother's legacy of artful self-expression lives on.

Not everyone is so blessed, of course—I've graded enough high school essays to know! Some people find it difficult to express themselves in speaking or writing, especially when it comes to expressing emotion. The entire greeting card industry is founded on the premise that people don't know how to say "I love you," or "I'm sorry," or "You have my sympathy," or even "Happy birthday!" There are even books with samples of letters for various occasions, and all you have to do is plug in the details.

But all arts and crafts are a form of self-expression, and baking is no different. You can say "I love you" to your family with a basket of warm onion buns. You might offer encouragement with a braided herb bread, or say "Welcome to the neighborhood!" with a pan of homemade rolls. And sage dumplings with homemade chicken soup can express get well wishes far better than a cartoon greeting card. To adapt an expression from a florist's ad campaign, "Say it with flour!"

REFLECTION

# BLUE CHEESE WALNUT BREAD

Yield: 3 mini loaves.

2 cups **bread flour**, divided

1 package **FLEISCHMANN'S** RapidRise Yeast

1 teaspoon **granulated sugar**

1 teaspoon **salt**

1 cup **milk**

1 tablespoon **butter**

1 **egg**

³/₄ cup crumbled **blue cheese**

¹/₂ cup chopped **walnuts**

Combine 1 cup of the flour, yeast, sugar and salt in a medium bowl; stir to mix. Combine milk and butter in a saucepan; heat to 120 to 130 degrees. Pour milk mixture into flour mixture; stir until combined. Add egg; beat until smooth. Add the remaining 1 cup flour; stir until flour is completely incorporated. Beat vigorously for about 200 strokes. Let batter rest 10 minutes. Fold in cheese and walnuts.

Divide batter among 3 well-greased mini-loaf pans. Put pans in a warm, draft-free place and lightly cover all three with a single sheet of plastic wrap. Let rise 30 to 45 minutes, or until just below the rim of the pans.

Bake in a preheated 350-degree oven 35 to 40 minutes, or until a wooden pick inserted in the center of the loaf comes out clean. Because of the cheese, the tops of the loaves will brown before the bread is fully baked, so after about 25 minutes of baking, loosely cover the tops of the loaves with foil. Let cool in pans on wire racks 20 minutes, then remove from pans and place on wire racks to cool completely.

*Note: I have made this bread in a molded loaf pan with a braided motif (7-cup size), as well as in flower pots especially manufactured for baking. Because it's a batter bread, you could use muffin tins or brioche molds as well, but you would have to reduce the baking time for smaller loaves.*

*Don't remove the bread from the pans too soon. The loaves take awhile to firm up and will deflate if you remove them from the pans while they are still hot.*

## Bread Break

Not everyone likes the flavor of blue cheese, but the people who do *really* like it! Because a number of my brethren at St. Bede are among the latter category, I developed this recipe as a lunch buffet treat. It's excellent with fresh fruit, especially pears. If you are particularly fond of blue cheese, you can increase the amount to a full cup, but be sure to break up larger clumps, or else the loaf won't hold together.

# Magic Caterpillar Peanut Butter Bread

Yield: 1 loaf.

## Bread Break

Most younger children love to be asked to help in the kitchen, especially if the project involves frosting! If you don't think your child is ready for a full-scale bread-baking lesson, you can enlist him or her in the decorating phase of bread making. This recipe for Magic Caterpillar Peanut Butter Bread is a fun project for a rainy day when there's nothing to do, or for a birthday party activity that will keep kids entertained while producing some of the treats. I recommend working with a small group of kids (five would work, but would be a bit crowded) or have one or two kids helping in the kitchen while others are doing something else.

Decorating foods with frosting is a long-standing tradition in my family. Every year at Christmas my mother would employ us to decorate the dozens of cut-out sugar cookies she baked for

1 package **FLEISCHMANN'S Active Dry Yeast**

$^1/_4$ cup lukewarm **water**

1 cup **milk**

$^3/_4$ cup **chunky peanut butter**

$^1/_4$ cup **granulated sugar**

1 teaspoon **salt**

$3^1/_4$ to $3^1/_2$ cups **all-purpose flour**, divided

**For decoration:** tubes of colored frosting, candies, gumdrops, licorice, etc.

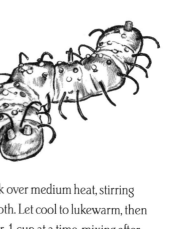

Sprinkle yeast over lukewarm water in large bowl; stir to dissolve yeast. Let stand about 10 minutes, or until foamy.

Combine milk, peanut butter, sugar and salt in small saucepan. Cook over medium heat, stirring constantly, until mixture is smooth. Let cool to lukewarm, then add to yeast mixture. Stir in flour, 1 cup at a time, mixing after each addition until flour is thoroughly incorporated.

Turn out dough onto lightly floured surface. Knead 5 minutes, adding small amounts of the remaining flour as needed to keep dough manageable. Rinse and dry bowl, then lightly oil surface of dough and place dough in bowl. Cover with a dry cloth and let rise in a warm, draft-free place 1 hour.

Punch down dough. Knead briefly to expel large air bubbles. Roll dough into a rope about 24 inches long. Form rope into a large S shape on a lightly greased 18x12-inch baking sheet. Using a butter knife or dough scraper, chop rope into 3-inch sections, but do not separate completely. Cover with a cloth and let rise about 30 minutes. (The caterpillar will magically grow back together during rising and baking.)

About 15 minutes before end of rising time, preheat oven to 375 degrees. Bake loaf 25 minutes, or until top is golden brown. Let cool on baking sheet 15 minutes, then carefully transfer to a wire rack to cool completely.

Decorate cooled loaf with frosting and gumdrops or other candy. Poke holes in the sides with a wooden pick and insert sections of licorice for legs.

≈

*Note: Decorating gel doesn't work as well as frosting does as a glue for the candy decorations, so make sure you pick up the right tube at the store. Any candies will work to make spots for the caterpillar's sections. Thin red licorice makes the perfect legs and antennae, unless you know your youngsters prefer the flavor of black licorice.*

our family as well as for gifts. One year Mom baked angel-shaped cookies for all her friends, and my sister Eileen and I decorated them to resemble each lady. She had intended for them to be eaten, but several of her friends were so taken with their cookie "portraits" that they saved them. That was over 25 years ago, and I know of at least one of Mom's friends who brings out her angel cookie every year to hang on the Christmas tree.

# MAGIC CATERPILLAR PEANUT BUTTER BREAD

Yield: 1 loaf.

1 cup **milk**

$^1/_4$ cup plus 3 tablespoons **water**

$^3/_4$ cup **chunky peanut butter**

1 teaspoon **salt**

3 cups **bread flour**

$^1/_4$ cup **granulated sugar**

2 teaspoons **FLEISCHMANN'S Bread Machine Yeast**

**For decoration:** colored frosting, candies, gumdrops, licorice, etc.

Add milk, water, peanut butter, salt, bread flour, sugar and yeast to bread machine pan in the order suggested by manufacturer. Select **dough/manual cycle**.

When cycle is complete, remove dough from bread machine. Roll dough into a 24-inch rope. Form rope into a large S shape on greased baking sheet. Using a butter knife or dough scraper, chop rope into 3-inch sections, but do not separate completely. Cover and let rise in a warm, draft-free place about 30 minutes, or until almost doubled.

Bake in a preheated 375-degree oven 20 to 25 minutes, or until done. Let cool on baking sheet 15 minutes, then carefully remove from sheet and place on wire rack to cool completely.

Decorate with frosting, gumdrops or candy. Poke holes in the sides with a wooden pick; insert sections of licorice for legs.

# Apple Spice Cake

Yield: 16 to 24 servings.

2 **eggs**

1 cup **vegetable oil**, such as canola

1/2 cup **milk**

1 teaspoon **vanilla extract**

1 cup **granulated sugar**

1/2 cup packed **brown sugar**

2 1/2 cups **whole wheat pastry flour**

2 teaspoons **ground cinnamon**

1/4 teaspoon **ground mace** or **nutmeg**

1 1/2 teaspoons **baking powder**

1/2 teaspoon **salt**

4 cups peeled, diced **apples**

1 cup chopped **nuts** (walnuts or pecans)

Combine eggs, oil, milk and vanilla in small bowl; stir until mixed. Sift granulated sugar, brown sugar, pastry flour, cinnamon, mace, baking powder and salt into a large bowl. Add egg mixture to flour mixture; mix well. Stir in apples and nuts. Pour batter into a lightly greased 13x9x2-inch baking pan. Bake in a preheated 350-degree oven 40 to 45 minutes, or until a toothpick inserted in center of cake comes out clean. Let cake cool in pan on wire rack 15 minutes before cutting.

≈

*Note: Other apple cake recipes of this size call for 1 cup each granulated and brown sugar, but I think that much sugar overwhelms the apple flavor, so I reduced it. If you prefer, you can substitute raw sugar, which is less processed than granulated sugar but has the same sweetening power.*

*I use organic whole wheat pastry flour because I prefer it to all-purpose flour for this recipe. Pastry flour is made from softer wheat than all-purpose or bread flour, so it makes lighter cakes and pie crusts. The whole wheat gives the cake a heartier flavor and texture, so it's a perfect choice for this recipe. In a pinch, any organic wheat flour will do, but your results will vary.*

## Bread Break

This spicy apple cake is the perfect way to warm up a chilly kitchen in late autumn. I developed this recipe last fall because our abbey orchard was producing some exquisite Lura Red apples, which are my favorite apple for baking or eating. Any firm, slightly tart apple will do, such as Granny Smith or Northern Spy. Ask your grocer for advice.

You might also consider using a higher quality of cinnamon such as Vietnamese or Korintje from Indonesia. My friend Stephanie gave me bottles of three different gourmet cinnamons and my monastic community has really noticed the difference in my baking.

This cake is excellent served warm. It also keeps well and can be baked a day ahead of time for a special dinner or potluck.

# HERBAL ENCOURAGEMENT BREAD

Yield: 1 loaf.

## Bread Break

I developed this recipe as a bread to share with a friend who is going through a difficult time. Several of the ingredients have a symbolic meaning. The sour cream symbolizes making the best of something that has gone bad. The onions represent tears. Thyme is the herb of perseverance and courage, as this hardy plant thrives in the rockiest and harshest of environments. The loaf is braided to suggest that although things in the person's life might look tangled and confused, stepping back and reflecting might reveal both a pattern and a purpose. A fresh loaf of homemade bread with a handwritten note explaining its message would mean far more than any store-bought card.

The first time I baked this bread, it was one of those cool evenings in mid-spring when you leave the windows of the kitchen open. You could actually smell the aroma of this bread all the way out in the parking lot by the school gym!

1 package **FLEISCHMANN'S Active Dry Yeast**

$^1/_4$ cup lukewarm **water**

1 (8-ounce) carton **sour cream**

1 **egg**

1 tablespoon **vegetable oil**

2 teaspoons **honey**

$^1/_4$ teaspoon **baking soda**

1 teaspoon **salt**

$^1/_4$ cup minced **onion**

$^1/_2$ teaspoon **dried thyme**

4 to 4 $^1/_2$ cups **all-purpose unbleached flour**, divided

Melted **butter**, for brushing on loaf (optional)

Dissolve yeast in lukewarm water in small bowl. Let stand 10 minutes, or until foamy.

Heat sour cream in a saucepan or microwave oven to 110 to 120 degrees. Pour warm sour cream into medium bowl. Add egg, oil, honey, baking soda, salt, onion and thyme; stir until thoroughly mixed. Add yeast mixture; stir to mix. Add 4 cups of the flour, 1 cup at a time, mixing thoroughly after each addition.

Turn out dough onto lightly floured surface. Knead gently 1 minute. Let dough rest 10 minutes; this resting period helps the dough to firm up. Knead 4 minutes, adding small amounts of remaining flour as needed to keep dough manageable. The dough will be elastic but slightly sticky. Rinse and dry bowl, then oil surface of dough and place dough in bowl. Cover with a cloth and let rise in a warm, draft-free place about 1 hour, or until doubled.

Punch down dough. Knead briefly to expel large air bubbles. Divide dough into 3 equal pieces. Roll each piece into an 18-inch rope. Braid the ropes to form a loaf; tuck the ends underneath. Place loaf on lightly greased baking sheet. Cover and let rise about 30 minutes, or until doubled.

About 15 minutes before end of rising time, preheat oven to 350 degrees. Bake loaf 25 to 30 minutes, or until golden brown and bread sounds hollow when tapped. Remove from baking sheet and let cool on wire rack 15 minutes, then brush top and sides of loaf with melted butter, if desired.

≈

*Note: Feel free to substitute sugar or molasses for honey in this recipe, according to personal taste. The chopped onion could be red, yellow, white or green, depending upon what's in the fridge. I usually saute onions before adding them to bread dough, but if you mince them fine, the raw onion may be added directly to the dough.*

# HERBAL ENCOURAGEMENT BREAD

Yield: 1 loaf.

$^{1}/_{4}$ cup **water**

1 (8-ounce) carton **sour cream**

1 **egg**

2 $^{1}/_{4}$ teaspoons **vegetable oil**

1 $^{1}/_{2}$ teaspoons **honey**

$^{3}/_{4}$ teaspoon **salt**

3 cups **bread flour**

$^{1}/_{8}$ teaspoon **baking soda**

2 tablespoons minced **onion**

$^{1}/_{3}$ teaspoon **dried thyme**

2 teaspoons **FLEISCHMANN'S Bread Machine Yeast**

Melted **butter** or **margarine**, for brushing on loaf (optional)

Add water, sour cream, egg, oil, honey, salt, bread flour, baking soda, onion, thyme and yeast to bread machine pan in the order suggested by manufacturer. Select **dough/manual cycle**.

When cycle is complete, remove dough from machine. Cover and let rest 10 minutes. Divide dough into 3 equal pieces. Roll each piece into an 18-inch rope. Braid ropes to form a loaf; tuck ends underneath. Place loaf on greased baking sheet. Cover and let rise in a warm, draft-free place about 45 minutes, or until doubled.

Bake in preheated 350-degree oven 20 to 25 minutes, or until done. Remove from baking sheet and let cool on wire rack. Brush top with melted butter, if desired.

≈

# ONION ROLLS

Yield: 8 large rolls.

$^1/_4$ cup **granulated sugar**

1 to 2 teaspoons **salt,** to taste

1 package **FLEISCHMANN'S RapidRise Yeast**

3 $^3/_4$ to 4 $^1/_4$ cups **all-purpose flour**, divided

$^3/_4$ cup **milk**

$^1/_2$ cup **water**

2 tablespoons **vegetable oil**

$^1/_4$ cup minced **onion**

**Milk**, for brushing tops of rolls

2 tablespoons minced **onion**, for topping

Combine sugar, salt, yeast and 2 cups of the flour in large bowl; stir until well mixed. Combine milk and water in small saucepan; heat to 120 to 130 degrees. Pour milk mixture into flour mixture; stir rapidly 2 minutes. Stir in oil and $^1/_4$ cup onion. Add 1 $^1/_2$ cups of the flour; mix until flour is thoroughly incorporated. Add remaining flour, about 2 tablespoons at a time, until you have a soft dough that is rather sticky but not unmanageable.

Turn out dough onto a lightly floured surface. Knead 5 minutes. Lightly dust your hands with flour to keep the dough from sticking as you knead. Do not add too much flour; you want a soft dough for these rolls. Cover dough with a damp cloth and let rest 10 minutes.

Divide dough into 8 equal pieces. Roll each piece into a rope about 16 inches long. For each roll, tie an overhand knot, leaving a 4-inch "tail." Twist the loop right over left, then tuck the tail under the roll and put it through the bottom loop. Place rolls, evenly spaced, on lightly greased 15x10-inch baking sheet or jelly-roll pan. Cover with a clean, dry cloth and let rise in a warm,

draft-free place about 1 hour, or until doubled.

About 15 minutes before end of rising time, preheat oven to 400 degrees. Using a soft pastry brush, lightly brush rolls with milk and sprinkle with 2 tablespoons onion; press onion gently into dough. Bake 15 to 20 minutes, or until browned. Remove from baking sheet and let cool on wire racks.

# ONION ROLLS

Yield: 8 rolls.

$^{1}/_{4}$ cup plus 3 tablespoons **water**

$^{1}/_{4}$ cup plus 2 tablespoons **milk**

1 teaspoon **salt**

2 cups **bread flour**

2 tablespoons minced **onion**

2 tablespoons **granulated sugar**

1 $^{1}/_{2}$ teaspoons **FLEISCHMANN'S Bread Machine Yeast**

**Milk**, for brushing tops of rolls

1 tablespoon minced **onion,** for topping

Add water, milk, salt, bread flour, 2 tablespoons onion, sugar and yeast to bread machine pan in the order suggested by manufacturer. Select **dough/manual cycle.**

When cycle is complete, remove dough from machine. Cover and let rest 10 minutes. Divide dough into 8 equal pieces. Shape each piece into a smooth ball. Place balls on greased baking sheet. Cover and let rise in a warm, draft-free place about 1 hour, or until doubled in size.

Brush rolls lightly with milk and sprinkle with 1 tablespoon onion, pressing onion gently into dough. Bake in a preheated 400-degree oven 10 minutes, or until done. Remove from baking sheet and let cool on wire rack.

# SPICY DATE NUT BREAD

Yield: 1 large loaf or 2 small loaves.

## Bread Break

If you like the aroma and flavor of anise, you'll love Chinese five spice powder. It's a blend of star anise, Szechuan pepper, fennel, cloves and cinnamon, and it's available in the spice rack of most large supermarkets. A lot of people use it to flavor stir-fried chicken, but it gives a unique flavor to breads, as well. In this recipe, Chinese five spice powder beautifully complements the sweetness of the dates, and the pecans add both flavor and texture to the loaf. If you are a little leery of the scent, use only 2 teaspoons the first time you make the bread, and increase it according to taste. If you can't find Chinese five spice powder, substitute 1/4 teaspoon ground cloves, 1 teaspoon ground cinnamon and 1 teaspoon either fennel seeds or ground anise.

As I do with most breads, I tested this one several times. During one of the trials, I was making kaiser rolls at the same time. Brother Nathaniel came down to the kitchen for a snack and

1 package **FLEISCHMANN'S Active Dry Yeast**

1 1/4 cups lukewarm **water**

1/2 cup **whole wheat flour**

2 tablespoons **brown sugar**

1 teaspoon **salt**

2 tablespoons **vegetable oil**

1 tablespoon **Chinese five spice powder**

1 **egg**

3 1/2 to 4 cups **bread flour**, divided

1 cup chopped **dates**

1/2 cup chopped **pecans**

Sprinkle yeast over lukewarm water in medium bowl; stir until yeast is completely dissolved. Add whole wheat flour, brown sugar, salt, oil, Chinese five spice powder and egg; stir until thoroughly mixed. Add 3 cups of the bread flour, 1 cup at a time, mixing after each addition until flour is completely incorporated. Add enough of the remaining bread flour, about 1/4 cup at a time, to form a soft dough.

Turn out dough onto lightly floured surface. Knead 6 to 8 minutes. Rinse and dry the bowl, then oil surface of dough and place in bowl. Cover with a clean, dry cloth and let rise in a warm, draft-free place about 1 hour, or until doubled.

Punch down dough. Let rest 5 minutes. Flatten dough into a rough oval about 1/2-inch thick. Place dates and pecans on dough and fold sides of dough over to enclose them. Knead dough to incorporate dates and nuts; at first the dough will be messy and seem to be falling apart, but be patient—it will all come together! Form dough into one large free-form loaf or two smaller loaves. If there are dates on the surface of the loaf, push them into the dough so they won't burn. Place loaf on a lightly greased baking sheet and let rise 30 to 45 minutes, or until nearly doubled.

About 15 minutes before the end of rising time, preheat oven to 375 degrees. Place on middle rack and bake 40 to 45 minutes (a bit less for two small loaves), or until crust is browned and loaf sounds hollow when tapped on the bottom. Remove from pan and let cool on wire rack.

⤳

*Note: When I make this for my monastic community at St. Bede, I let the loaf rise the second time in a French banneton (also called a brotform in German), which is a tightly coiled basket. I generously dust the interior with flour, then place the dough in the basket to rise. When it has doubled, I place a baking sheet on top of the basket and flip the basket over. The risen dough drops out of the basket onto the baking sheet, and the spiral pattern of the basket appears in flour on the top of the loaf. The pattern becomes even more pronounced as the crust browns. I use a round banneton, but they make long oval ones as well.*

immediately pounced on one of the fresh rolls. Because of the Chinese five spice powder in this bread, the kitchen was filled with the aroma of anise, a seasoning his mother used often in her holiday baking. Before he went to bed, he thanked me "not only for a delicious roll, but for a wonderful scent from my memories."

# SPICY DATE NUT BREAD

Yield: 1 (1 ¹/₂-pound) loaf.

³/₄ cup **water**

1 tablespoon **vegetable oil**

1 **egg**

¹/₂ teaspoon **salt**

2 cups **bread flour**

¹/₄ cup **whole wheat flour**

¹/₂ cup chopped **dates**

¹/₂ cup chopped **pecans**

1 tablespoon **brown sugar**

1 ¹/₂ teaspoons **Chinese five spice powder**

1 ¹/₂ teaspoons **FLEISCHMANN'S Bread Machine Yeast**

Add water, oil, egg, salt, bread flour, whole wheat flour, dates, pecans, brown sugar, Chinese five spice powder and yeast to bread machine pan in the order suggested by manufacturer. Select **basic cycle; medium/normal color setting**.

⤳

Yield: 16 rolls.

## Bread Break

Nothing says "Welcome to the neighborhood" like a loaf of freshly baked bread or a pan of homemade rolls. These rolls are flavored with herbs that symbolize some of the qualities of a happy home, so bake them for a new neighbor or for an old friend settling into a new house.

Parsley was served between courses at Roman feasts; chewing the leaves helped cleanse the palate and sweeten the breath. Thus parsley came to be associated with hospitality and partying. I'm not sure how the other herbs obtained their meanings, but I do have some speculation. Marjoram may signify joy because of its cheerful flowers, which are among the earliest herbal blooms in the spring. Sage is an appropriate symbol of longevity, as sage plants can live for decades, and the leaves may be harvested for use well into the winter, after other plants have died back completely. I suspect rosemary may be the herb of

1 recipe **Single Loaf White Bread dough** (page 28)

¹/₄ cup (¹/₂ stick) **butter**, melted

1 tablespoon **dried parsley flakes** (for merriment and hospitality)

1 teaspoon **dried marjoram** (for joy)

¹/₂ teaspoon **dried rubbed sage** (for health and long life)

¹/₂ teaspoon **dried rosemary leaves**, crushed (for good memories)

**Milk** and **sesame seeds**, for topping (optional)

Prepare dough for Single Loaf White Bread through the first rising. Punch down dough and knead briefly to expel large air bubbles. Divide dough into 16 equal pieces and form each piece into a ball (about the size of a walnut).

Combine melted butter, parsley, marjoram, sage and rosemary in small bowl; stir to mix. Dip each ball of dough in butter mixture, then arrange balls in a single layer in an ungreased 2-quart baking dish. Pour remaining butter mixture over balls. Cover with plastic wrap and let rise in a warm, draft-free place about 30 minutes, or until doubled.

About 15 minutes before end of rising time, preheat oven to 350 degrees. Remove plastic wrap. If desired, brush tops of rolls with milk and sprinkle with sesame seeds. Bake 20 to 25 minutes, or until browned on top and rolls begin to pull slightly away from sides of dish. Let cool in baking dish on wire rack 10 minutes, then remove rolls from baking dish and place on wire rack to cool.

❧

*Note: If you think the rolls are browning too quickly, loosely cover them with aluminum foil, then remove foil for last 5 or 10 minutes of baking. The sesame seeds really do add to the appearance, so if you have them on hand, by all means use them.*

*For the sake of convenience, I have used dried herbs for this recipe. If you use fresh herbs, use double the amounts of parsley and marjo-*

*ram, but only ³/₄ teaspoon each of fresh minced sage and rosemary. These stronger herbs can be overwhelming when fresh. I use Bergarten sage and Huntington Carpet rosemary varieties, but the more ordinary officinalis forms can be used with the same results.*

remembrance because it retains its strong, piney scent for so long after harvesting.

# HOUSEWARMING ROLLS

Yield: 16 rolls.

1 cup **milk**

¹/₃ cup **water**

1 tablespoon **vegetable oil**

1 **egg**

1 teaspoon **salt**

3 ¹/₄ cups **bread flour**

1 tablespoon **granulated sugar**

2 teaspoons **FLEISCHMANN'S Bread Machine Yeast**

¹/₄ cup (¹/₂ stick) **butter** or **margarine**, melted

1 tablespoon **dried parsley flakes**

1 teaspoon **dried marjoram**

¹/₂ teaspoon **dried rubbed sage**

¹/₂ teaspoon **dried rosemary leaves**, crushed

**Milk** and **sesame seeds**, for topping (optional)

Add milk, water, oil, egg, salt, bread flour, sugar and yeast to bread machine in the order suggested by manufacturer. Select **dough/ manual cycle**.

When cycle is complete, remove dough from machine to a lightly floured surface. Cover and let rest 10 minutes. Divide dough into 16 equal pieces; roll each piece into a ball.

Combine melted butter, parsley, marjoram, sage and rosemary in small bowl; stir to mix. Dip each ball into butter mixture; arrange balls in single layer in ungreased 2-quart baking dish. Pour remaining butter mixture over balls. Cover and let rise in a warm, draft-free place about 45 minutes, or until doubled.

If desired, brush tops of rolls with milk and sprinkle with sesame seeds. Bake in a preheated 350-degree oven 25 to 30 minutes, or until done. Let cool in baking dish on wire rack 10 minutes, then remove from dish and let cool on wire rack.

# Sage Dumplings

Yield: About 1 dozen.

## Bread Break

I was a bit afraid of attempting dumplings for many years because they are a bread cooked in liquid rather than baked in an oven. But once I discovered how easy they are (and how delicious), I became a dumpling devotee.

Dumplings go well with many kinds of soups, especially those made with stock or broth. Feel free to experiment with other herbs to complement the flavors of your soup. I like rosemary and thyme dumplings with a thick beef soup or stew; marjoram and chives complement vegetable soups.

Sage symbolizes health and longevity. I haven't found an official explanation for its traditional meaning, but I do know that you can harvest fresh sage well into the winter. I brush the snow off my sage plants in November and collect leaves for Thanksgiving stuffing. If the plants stay healthy that long, they must have some health-bearing properties!

1 cup **all-purpose flour**

1 teaspoon **salt**

¹/₄ teaspoon **dried ground sage**

2 teaspoons **baking powder**

1 **egg**

¹/₄ cup **milk**

1 (46-ounce) can **chicken broth** (or about 1 ¹/₂ quarts homemade)

Sift flour, salt, sage and baking powder into large bowl; stir to mix. In another bowl, combine egg and milk; mix lightly with a fork. Add egg mixture to flour mixture; mix just until moistened.

Using two soup spoons, scoop about 2 tablespoons batter and wipe from the bowl of one spoon to the other until you have formed a ball; place ball on parchment paper or a plate. Repeat until all batter is formed into balls.

Drop balls into a pot of simmering chicken broth. The dumplings will float on top as they cook. Cover pot with a lid in order to steam the dumplings (a glass lid or inverted glass pie plate is helpful so you can watch the dumplings cook). After 5 minutes, check dumplings every minute until they are done. The dumplings are done when a wooden pick inserted in center comes out clean.

Serve dumplings with chicken broth as a simple, nourishing soup. Or, cook the dumplings in Chicken Soup (page 119) for a heartier version, as an herbal get-well to a sick friend.

*Note: The amount of sage in this recipe is quite small for two reasons: the recipe is meant for someone who is sick and might not be able to tolerate strong flavors, and sage can be overpowering in any recipe, so it's best to go easy. Use no more than ¹/₂ teaspoon even for the healthiest diner!*

# WORLD HERITAGE BREADS

When I first joined the monastery, I had a fairly limited repertoire of bread recipes: French baguettes, basic white, whole wheat, pull-apart garlic bread, raisin bread and crescent rolls. Oh, I could bake Irish soda bread, and I had watched my mom make cinnamon rolls often enough that I knew I could produce a decent batch, but other than that, my baking was pretty basic.

My third summer at the abbey, I received permission to plant a small herb garden. But what to do with all that sage and thyme and rosemary? So I began adding herbs to my basic recipes, and my baking horizons began to expand. But the real impetus for my becoming a truly knowledgeable baker came from an unexpected source—my fellow monks.

The monks at St. Bede, like those at most monasteries, come from a variety of backgrounds. Some have lived in the Illinois Valley all their lives, others are from more distant cities and towns in Illinois, still others have found their way to the abbey from Ohio or Maryland or North Dakota. And we come from a variety of ethnic backgrounds as well. Father Philip is Italian, Brother Nathaniel has relatives in Alsace, Brother George is Japanese, and Abbot Roger's father was Lithuanian and Irish, and his mother was Polish. German or Slovenian heritage is also common among the brethren.

And all of those cultures have their unique breads, both festal and ferial. Once I became the unofficial baker of the community, notes from my confreres started appearing in my mailbox: "You might want to try this—it's my grandmother's," and a photocopied recipe card would be attached. Our beekeeper, Father Arthur, started sharing recipes using honey, and Father Ronald got me hooked on experimenting with pizza and other breads like the ones he enjoyed while studying in Rome. Before long I had to start entering my recipes on the computer and keep them organized in a three-ring binder.

My brothers' encouragement has served not only as the impetus for the breads in this chapter, but for the whole television series as well. It is to them that I owe my deepest thanks.

# Paska

Yield: 1 loaf.

### Sponge:

1 package **FLEISCHMANN'S Active Dry Yeast**

1 teaspoon **granulated sugar**

$^1/_4$ cup lukewarm **water**

1 cup lukewarm **milk**

2 cups **all-purpose flour**

### Dough:

3 **eggs**

$^1/_2$ cup **granulated sugar**

$^1/_4$ cup ($^1/_2$ stick) **butter**, melted

1 teaspoon **salt**

1 tablespoon freshly grated **orange peel**

$^1/_2$ teaspoon **almond extract**

1 cup **dried cherries** or **cranberries**

3 to 3 $^1/_2$ cups **all-purpose flour**, divided

Your favorite **confectioners' sugar frosting**, warmed (optional)

**Colored sugars** or other decorations (optional)

**For sponge:** Dissolve yeast and sugar in lukewarm water in large bowl. Add milk and flour; beat until smooth. Cover and let stand 1 hour, or until foamy and doubled in volume.

**For dough:** Add eggs, sugar, melted butter and salt to sponge; beat well. Add orange peel, almond extract and dried cherries; beat until well mixed. Add 2 cups of the flour; beat until flour is thoroughly incorporated. Add 1 cup of the flour; beat until thoroughly incorporated.

Turn out dough onto lightly floured surface. Knead 5 minutes, adding small amounts of remaining flour as needed to keep the dough manageable. Dough should be soft and slightly sticky, but smooth and elastic. Lightly oil the surface of the dough and place it in a clean, dry bowl. Cover and let rise in a warm, draft-free place 60 to 90 minutes, or until doubled.

Punch down dough. Knead briefly. Shape dough into a smooth ball. Grease a clean 2-pound coffee can with solid vegetable shortening. Place dough in can. Cover and let rise 30 to 45 min-

## Bread Break

This bread is traditionally served at Easter by the Ukrainian Mennonites, who borrowed the shape from their Orthodox neighbors. The domed top is meant to suggest the domes of Orthodox churches. Often the top of the loaf is decorated with elaborate shapes made of dough, usually with a cross in the center. These specially decorated paska loaves are taken to church on Easter morning, along with colored eggs and other Easter foods, usually in a special basket decorated with ribbons and flowers. While the choir sings the traditional Ukrainian Easter hymn "Christ Is Risen," the priest blesses the baskets for the congregation.

This is, I must admit, my own version of paska, and therefore a nontraditional recipe. A more authentic version would use raisins soaked in rum, lemon peel and vanilla bean, in comparable proportions to the cherries, orange peel and almond extract in my recipe.

utes, or until nearly doubled.

About 15 minutes before end of rising time, preheat oven to 350 degrees. Bake loaf 40 to 50 minutes, or until top is browned and the loaf is just

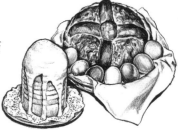

beginning to pull away from the sides of the can. If you have an instant-read thermometer, the interior temperature of the loaf should be between 190 and 195 degrees.

Let cool in can on wire rack 20 to 30 minutes, then carefully slide loaf from can and stand loaf upright on wire rack to cool completely. If desired, before serving, top with warmed frosting and let it drip down the sides. Sprinkle with colored sugar or other decorations.

⌇

**Note:** *If you don't have a coffee can, you can bake this bread in two 8 $^1$/$_2$ x4 $^1$/$_2$ x2 $^1$/$_2$-inch loaf pans.*

# PASKA

Yield: 1 (1 $^1$/$_2$-pound) loaf.

$^1$/$_2$ cup **milk**

$^1$/$_4$ cup **water**

2 tablespoons **butter** or **margarine**

1 **egg**

$^1$/$_4$ teaspoon **almond extract**

$^1$/$_2$ teaspoon **salt**

2 $^1$/$_2$ cups **bread flour**

$^1$/$_2$ cup **dried cranberries**

$^1$/$_4$ cup **granulated sugar**

1 $^1$/$_2$ teaspoons **grated orange peel**

2 teaspoons **FLEISCHMANN'S Bread Machine Yeast**

Add milk, water, butter, egg, almond extract, salt, bread flour, cranberries, sugar, orange peel and yeast to bread machine pan in the order suggested by manufacturer, adding cranberries with flour. Select **basic/white bread cycle; medium/normal color setting**.

⌇

# Red Onion Focaccia

Yield: 1 (9-inch) focaccia.

## Dough:

1 package **FLEISCHMANN'S Active Dry Yeast**

1 cup lukewarm **water**

1 tablespoon **olive oil**

1 teaspoon **salt**

3 to 3 1/2 cups **all-purpose flour**, divided

**Cornmeal**, for sprinkling peel

## Topping:

**Olive oil**, for brushing

1 small **red onion**, thinly sliced

3 tablespoons **olive oil**

1/2 teaspoon **coarse salt**

Sprinkle yeast over lukewarm water in medium bowl; stir to dissolve. Add oil and salt. Add 1 cup of the flour; beat until smooth. Repeat with 1 cup flour. Add enough of the remaining flour, 1/4 cup at a time, to form a soft dough.

Turn out dough onto lightly floured surface. Knead 6 to 8 minutes. Rinse and dry bowl, then oil surface of dough and place in bowl. Cover with a clean, dry cloth and let rise in a warm, draft-free place about 1 hour, or until doubled.

Punch down dough. On a lightly floured surface, pat or roll dough into a circle 8 or 9 inches across. Place on a peel that has been sprinkled with cornmeal. Cover and let rise 20 minutes.

Place a pizza stone on middle shelf of oven. Preheat oven to 400 degrees. (The stone needs to preheat at least 30 minutes.)

With fingertip, dimple surface of the dough (make indentations) at 1-inch intervals. Lightly brush surface of dough with olive oil. Toss onion slices with 3 tablespoons olive oil; spread onion mixture on dough. Sprinkle with coarse salt. Let rise 10 minutes. Slide loaf off peel and onto pizza stone; bake in 400-degree oven 25 to 30 minutes, or until golden. Remove from stone. Cut into wedges. Serve warm.

❧

*Note: If you don't have a pizza stone, place the loaf on a lightly greased baking sheet (the heavier the better) for the second rising, then continue*

## Bread Break

This recipe is a perfect example of how simple ingredients and method can combine to make something extraordinary. The dough is absolutely basic, the topping could hardly be easier, but the resulting loaf is far more than the sum of its ingredients. The first time I made this, Father Gabriel claimed it was "the best bread I've had in a very long time," and Father Ronald asked if I had "done something special with the crust."

*with the directions. You can use other kinds of onions with good results, but I think red onions look most attractive. If you can't find a small onion, use about half of a medium one. You can always use the remainder in a salad. Or better still, double this focaccia recipe!*

Bread Machine

# RED ONION FOCACCIA

Yield: 1 (9-inch) focaccia.

### DOUGH:

| | |
|---|---|
| 1 cup plus 2 tablespoons **water** | 1 $^1/_2$ teaspoons **FLEISCHMANN'S** Bread Machine Yeast |
| 1 tablespoon **olive oil** | |
| 1 teaspoon **salt** | **Cornmeal**, for sprinkling peel |
| 3 cups **bread flour** | |

### TOPPING:

| | |
|---|---|
| **Olive oil**, for brushing | 3 tablespoons **olive oil** |
| 1 small **red onion**, thinly sliced | $^1/_2$ teaspoon **coarse salt** |

Add water, olive oil, salt, bread flour and yeast to bread machine pan in the order suggested by manufacturer. Select **dough/manual cycle.**

When cycle is complete, remove dough from machine. Cover and let rest 10 minutes. Place a pizza stone on middle shelf of oven; preheat oven to 400 degrees.

On a lightly floured surface, roll dough to a 9-inch circle. Place on peel sprinkled with cornmeal. With fingertip, make indentations (dimples) in dough at 1-inch intervals. Cover and let rise in a warm, draft-free place 10 minutes.

Lightly brush dough with olive oil. Combine onion slices and 3 tablespoons olive oil; sprinkle over dough. Sprinkle with coarse salt. Slide loaf off peel and onto pizza stone; bake in 400-degree oven 25 to 30 minutes, or until golden. Remove from stone. Cut into wedges. Serve warm.

**Note:** *If you don't have a peel, place the loaf on a piece of parchment paper to rise. When ready to bake, transfer loaf on parchment paper to preheated pizza stone.*

# COTTAGE LOAF

Yield: 1 large loaf.

2 cups lukewarm **water**

2 packages **FLEISCHMANN'S Active Dry Yeast**

2 tablespoons **honey**

3 cups **whole wheat flour**

$^1/_4$ cup **nonfat dry milk powder**

1 tablespoon **vital wheat gluten**

3 tablespoons **vegetable oil**, such as canola

2 teaspoons **salt**

3 $^1/_2$ to 4 cups **bread flour**, divided

**Cornmeal**, for sprinkling on baking sheet

**Water** or **milk**, for brushing on dough

Combine lukewarm water, yeast and honey in large bowl; stir until yeast is completely dissolved. Add whole wheat flour, dry milk powder, gluten, oil and salt; stir until thoroughly mixed. Add 3 cups of the bread flour, 1 cup at a time, mixing after each addition until flour is completely incorporated. Work in enough of the remaining bread flour, about $^1/_4$ cup at a time, to form a fairly stiff dough.

Turn out dough onto floured surface. Knead 10 to 12 minutes. Rinse and dry the bowl, then oil the surface of the dough and place it in the bowl. Cover with a clean, dry cloth and let rise in a warm, draft-free place about 1 hour, or until doubled.

Punch down dough; let rest 5 minutes. Divide dough into two pieces, one about two-thirds of dough and the other about one-third of dough. Form each piece into a smooth ball. Place balls on lightly floured pan and cover with a clean, dry cloth. Let rise in a warm, draft-free place about 20 minutes.

Lightly grease a large baking sheet or jelly-roll pan and sprinkle it with cornmeal. Carefully place the large

## Bread Break

The cottage loaf shape can be used for any bread, wheat or white. The shape originated in Britain during the Roman occupation, when ovens were rather tall and shaped like beehives. To stack one loaf on top of another made maximum use of oven space, a necessity when the ovens were communal and had to accommodate all the bakers in the village.

I like to serve this loaf for supper by having the waiter deliver it, still warm, to the abbot's table. It makes quite a spectacular entrance! After the abbot and his tablemates (the prior and subprior) have taken their slices, it is passed from table to table, starting with the senior monks. Fortunately, the loaf is large enough that there's always some left by the time it reaches the junior table where I sit!

piece of dough in center of prepared baking sheet; lightly brush top of dough with water or milk. Place the small piece of dough on top; use two fingers or the floured end of a wooden spoon to push dough down in the center to make the two pieces stick together. Cover and let rise 20 minutes.

While dough is rising, preheat oven to 375 degrees. Bake bread 50 to 55 minutes, or until crust is browned and loaf sounds hollow when tapped on the bottom. Remove from baking sheet and let cool on wire rack.

*Note:* *I find it's best to bake this loaf by time rather than appearance. Often the surface browns quickly and even the "tap on the bottom" test makes you think the bread is done, but the loaf is so large it might still be doughy in the center. It won't hurt to leave the bread in the oven an extra five minutes, but taking it out too early might yield disappointing results.*

*You can slice this bread in any number of ways. Some people slice off the top piece and cut it into wedges first, then slice the bottom section. I like to use a "herringbone" slicing pattern, which makes the pieces a bit more manageable than slicing all the way across such a huge loaf.*

# Cottage Loaf

Bread Machine

Yield: 1 small loaf.

1 ¼ cups **water**

1 ½ tablespoons **vegetable oil**, such as canola

1 tablespoon **honey**

1 teaspoon **salt**

1 ½ cups **bread flour**

1 ½ cups **whole wheat flour**

2 tablespoons **nonfat dry milk powder**

1 tablespoon **vital wheat gluten**

2 teaspoons **FLEISCHMANN'S Bread Machine Yeast**

**Cornmeal**, for sprinkling on baking sheet

**Water** or **milk**, for brushing on dough

Add water, oil, honey, salt, bread flour, whole wheat flour, dry milk powder, gluten and yeast to bread machine pan in the order suggested by manufacturer. Select **dough/manual cycle**.

When cycle is complete, remove dough from machine. Divide dough into 2 pieces, one about two-thirds of dough and the other about one-third of dough. Form each piece into a smooth ball. Place balls on lightly floured pan. Cover and let rise in a warm, draft-free place 20 minutes.

Grease a baking sheet and sprinkle it with cornmeal. Carefully place large piece of dough on baking sheet. Lightly brush top of dough with water or milk. Place small piece of dough on top; use two fingers or the floured end of a wooden spoon to push down in the center to make the two pieces stick together. Cover and let rise 20 minutes.

Bake in a preheated 375-degree oven 25 to 30 minutes, or until done. Remove from baking sheet and let cool on wire rack.

# Vanocka

## Bread Break

I first encountered a recipe for *vanocka* in an issue of a women's magazine from 1956. It included holiday ethnic foods from all over the world—a real treasure trove of recipes! The mother of a high school classmate (and a devoted viewer) very kindly shared it with me, and I intend to bake my way across the globe this Christmas!

Vanocka is also called *hoska* or *stricka* in various places in the Czech Republic. The ingredients are somewhat variable. Sometimes this traditional Christmas braid contains candied citron or other dried fruits, more eggs, less sugar, different spices, etc. Truly expert bakers might make more complex braids out of multiple strands. One thing is constant: This loaf is as delicious in taste as it is dramatic in appearance. The monks of our abbey are happy to see this on the breakfast buffet any time of year!

2 packages **FLEISCHMANN'S Active Dry Yeast**

Pinch **granulated sugar**

$^1/_2$ cup lukewarm **water**

1 cup **milk**

$^1/_2$ cup (1 stick) **butter**

$^3/_4$ cup **granulated sugar**

2 teaspoons **salt**

1 tablespoon grated **lemon peel**

1 teaspoon **ground coriander**

$^1/_2$ teaspoon **ground mace** or **nutmeg**

2 **eggs**

1 **egg white** (use yolk for glaze)

6 $^1/_2$ to 7 cups **all-purpose flour**, divided

1 $^1/_2$ cups **golden raisins**

$^1/_2$ cup chopped **blanched almonds**

1 **egg yolk** beaten with $^1/_4$ cup **water**, for egg glaze

Combine yeast, pinch of sugar and lukewarm water in large bowl; stir until yeast is dissolved. Let stand about 15 minutes, or until foamy. Combine milk, butter, $^3/_4$ cup sugar and salt in small saucepan. Heat over medium heat, stirring frequently, until sugar is dissolved and butter is melted; let cool to lukewarm. Add milk mixture, lemon peel, coriander and mace to yeast mixture; stir until well mixed. Lightly beat 2 eggs and 1 egg white; add to yeast mixture and stir until well blended. Add 6 cups of the flour, 1 cup at a time, mixing after each addition until flour is thoroughly incorporated. Cover dough and let rest 10 minutes.

Turn out dough onto a lightly floured surface. Knead dough about 5 minutes, adding remaining flour, about $^1/_4$ cup at a time, until you get a soft dough that is smooth and elastic. Wash and dry the bowl, lightly oil surface of dough, and place dough in bowl. Cover with a dry cloth and let rise in a warm, draft-free place about 2 hours.

Punch down dough. Flatten into a rough oval about $^1/_2$-inch thick. Place raisins and almonds in center of dough and fold sides of dough over to enclose them. Knead dough until raisins and almonds are evenly distributed. Let dough rest 10 minutes.

Divide dough in half. Divide one half into 3 equal pieces; roll each piece into a rope about 16 inches long. Braid the three ropes together. Place on lightly greased 18x12 baking sheet. Divide the remaining half of dough into 5 equal pieces. Roll 3 of the pieces into ropes about 14 inches long; braid ropes together. Brush the top of the larger braid with water and place the smaller braid on top. Roll the remaining 2 pieces of dough into 12-inch ropes; twist ropes together. Brush the top of the smaller braid with water and place the twist on top. Insert wooden skewers vertically at both ends and in the center of loaf to keep braids and twist in place during rising and baking. Cover and let rise 45 to 60 minutes, or until nearly doubled.

About 15 minutes before end of rising time, preheat oven to 350 degrees. Use a soft pastry brush to brush surface of risen loaf with egg glaze. Place in middle third of oven and bake 45 to 55 minutes. If the surface starts to brown too quickly, cover it loosely with aluminum foil the last 15 minutes of baking. The loaf is fully baked when a cake tester inserted in the center comes out clean and the crust is a deep, rich brown. Let stand on baking sheet 15 minutes, then transfer to a wire rack to cool.

*Note: Be careful not to overknead the dough before the first rising, because it gets kneaded again. The raisins and almonds are added later to keep them from being pulverized from overhandling.*

*Cut the wooden skewers about 2 inches longer than the height of the loaf before rising. If they stick up any higher, they interfere with the cloth cover and can get caught on a rack in the oven and spoil the shape of the loaf. If you don't have skewers, use long tooth-picks. Or, divide dough into two portions, two-thirds of dough and one-third of dough, and make a two-layer braid (rather than three layers).*

*You can substitute 1 1/2 teaspoons lemon extract for the grated lemon peel. You might try replacing some or all of the raisins with chopped dried apricots. I have baked this bread without the traditional egg glaze and discovered that the golden yellow blush of the bread is more noticeable.*

Bread Machine

# VANOCKA

Yield: 1 loaf.

¹/₂ cup **milk**

¹/₄ cup **water**

¹/₄ cup (¹/₂ stick) **butter** or **margarine**

1 **egg**

1 **egg white** (use yolk for glaze)

1 teaspoon **salt**

3 cups plus 1 tablespoon **bread flour**

³/₄ cup **golden raisins**

¹/₄ cup chopped **almonds**

¹/₄ cup plus 2 tablespoons **granulated sugar**

1 ¹/₂ teaspoons **grated lemon peel**

¹/₂ teaspoon **ground coriander**

¹/₄ teaspoon **ground mace** or **nutmeg**

2 teaspoons **FLEISCHMANN'S Bread Machine Yeast**

1 **egg yolk** beaten with 1 tablespoon **water**, for egg glaze

Add milk, water, butter, egg, egg white, salt, bread flour, raisins, almonds, sugar, lemon peel, coriander, mace and yeast to bread machine pan in the order suggested by manufacturer. Select **dough/manual cycle.**

When cycle is complete, remove dough from machine. Cover and let rest 10 minutes. Divide dough in half. Divide one half into 3 equal pieces. Roll each piece into 16-inch rope; braid ropes together. Place braid on greased baking sheet. Divide remaining half of dough into 5 equal pieces. Roll 3 of the pieces into 14-inch ropes; braid ropes together. Brush top of larger braid with water; place smaller braid on top. Roll remaining 2 pieces of dough into 12-inch ropes; twist ropes together. Brush top of smaller braid with water; place twist on top. Insert wooden skewers at both ends and in the center of loaf to keep braids and twist in place during rising and baking. Cover and let rise in a warm, draft-free place about 1 hour, or until doubled.

Brush surface of risen loaf with egg glaze. Bake in a preheated 350-degree oven about 30 minutes, or until done. Let stand on baking sheet 15 minutes, then transfer to wire rack to cool.

# French Baguettes

Yield: 3 long skinny loaves.

1 package **FLEISCHMANN'S Active Dry Yeast**

2 1/2 cups lukewarm **water**

2 teaspoons **salt**

3 cups **bread flour**

3 to 3 1/2 cups **all-purpose flour**, divided

**Cornmeal**, for sprinkling on pan

1 **egg white** beaten with 2 tablespoons **water**, for egg wash (optional)

Dissolve yeast in lukewarm water in large bowl. Add salt and bread flour; beat until smooth. Cover bowl with plastic wrap and let yeast develop at room temperature for 3 hours. The batter will triple in volume and then begin to fall.

Uncover bowl and stir down batter. Add 3 cups of the all-purpose flour, 1 cup at a time, stirring after each addition until flour is thoroughly incorporated. Turn out dough onto a lightly floured surface. Knead 8 to 10 minutes, adding small amounts of remaining all-purpose flour as needed. The dough should be manageable, but still soft and rather moist. Rinse and dry the bowl, then oil the surface of the dough and place it in bowl. Cover and let rise in a warm, draft-free place about 1 hour, or until doubled.

Punch down dough. Knead briefly. Divide dough into three equal pieces. Roll each piece into an oval about 12x5 inches. Brush any excess flour off the top of the oval. Starting with a long edge, roll each oval into a cylinder. As you roll, pull the dough slightly to stretch it tight, so there are no air pockets. Pinch the seam to seal (if necessary, brush edge with water first).

Lightly grease an 18x12x1-inch baking pan; lightly sprinkle with cornmeal. Space loaves evenly, seam-side down, on prepared pan. Cover with a clean, dry cloth. Let rise 30 to 45 minutes, or until doubled.

About 30 minutes before baking, place a shallow pan containing 3/4 cup water on bottom shelf of oven. Preheat oven to 450 degrees.

If desired, brush risen loaves with egg wash. With a sharp knife or

## Bread Break

As many viewers know, French baguettes were my first bread baking project, back in the fifth grade. I've learned how to bake hundreds of different breads since then, but I continue to return to this old favorite. My fellow monks love this bread as much as my grade school classmates. Once I made six large baguettes for supper, and there was a bread bag filled with leftover slices. Father Philip came into the kitchen that evening looking for a snack and took the leftover bread back to the TV room with some white Cheddar cheese. He and Father Ambrose polished off the entire bag during the course of a Cubs-White Sox baseball game!

razor blade, slash long diagonal cuts in tops of loaves. Bake in 450-degree oven 25 to 30 minutes, or until done. (The breads could come out after as little as 20 minutes, but the longer baking time makes for a sturdier crust.) Remove from pan and let cool on wire racks. Baguettes are best if served the same day they are baked.

≈

**Note:** *The bread flour used at the beginning is able to stand up to the long process of a three-hour fermentation, and the all-purpose flour added later on makes for a softer interior. But if you have only one kind of flour in the house, make the loaves anyway.*

*Many baguette recipes recommend a 60-minute final rising, but every time I've let the loaves rise that long, they completely deflated when I slashed the tops and the resulting loaves weren't as light as I had hoped. If your kitchen is air conditioned, you might need that long, so experiment with different rising times. Remember, it's bread, it's going to forgive you!*

# French Baguettes

Yield: 2 loaves.

1 ⅓ cups **water**

1 teaspoon **salt**

1 ½ cups **bread flour**

1 ½ cups **all-purpose flour**

1 ½ teaspoons
   **FLEISCHMANN'S** Bread
   Machine Yeast

**Cornmeal**, for sprinkling on pan

1 **egg white** beaten with
   1 tablespoon **water**, for egg
   wash (optional)

Add water, salt, bread flour, all-purpose flour and yeast to bread machine pan in the order suggested by manufacturer. Select **dough/manual cycle**.

When cycle is complete, remove dough from machine and place on lightly floured surface. Cover and let rest 10 minutes. Divide dough into 2 equal pieces. Roll each piece into a 10x4-inch rectangle. Beginning with long end, tightly roll up each rectangle as for a jelly roll. Pinch seams and ends to seal.

Grease baking sheet and sprinkle with cornmeal. Place loaves, seam-side down, on baking sheet. Cover and let rise in warm, draft-free place about 1 hour, or until doubled. With a sharp knife, slash tops diagonally. If desired, brush loaves with egg wash.

Place a shallow pan containing ¾ cup water on bottom shelf of oven; preheat oven to 450 degrees. Bake loaves about 20 minutes, or until done. Remove from baking sheet and let cool on wire rack.

# KAISER ROLLS

Yield: 12 rolls.

2 packages
**FLEISCHMANN'S Active Dry Yeast**

1 cup lukewarm **water**

1 tablespoon **barley malt syrup** (see note)

1 cup lukewarm **milk**

1 tablespoon **vegetable oil**

1 tablespoon **salt**

1 **egg yolk**

6 to 6 $\frac{1}{2}$ cups **all-purpose flour**, divided

2 tablespoons **cornmeal**, for sprinkling on pan

1 **egg white** beaten with 2 tablespoons **water**, for egg wash

**Sesame** or **poppy seeds**, for topping (optional)

Sprinkle yeast over lukewarm water in large bowl; stir until yeast is completely dissolved. Stir in malt syrup; let stand 10 minutes. Add milk, oil, salt and egg yolk; stir until thoroughly mixed. Add 6 cups of the flour, 1 cup at a time, mixing after each addition until flour is completely incorporated.

Turn out dough onto lightly floured surface. Knead 6 to 8 minutes, adding small amounts of the remaining flour as needed to keep the dough manageable. Rinse and dry bowl, then oil surface of dough and place in bowl. Cover with a clean, dry cloth and let rise in a warm, draft-free place about 1 hour, or until doubled.

Punch down dough. Knead briefly to expel large air bubbles. Divide dough into 12 equal pieces. Lightly grease an 18x12-inch baking sheet; sprinkle with cornmeal. Roll each piece of dough into a ball, then flatten ball into a circle 3 to 4 inches across. Dust surface of dough lightly with flour to keep it from sticking to your hands. Place rolls, evenly spaced, on prepared baking sheet. Cover with a clean, dry cloth and let rise 20 minutes.

Remove cloth. Press each roll firmly with a kaiser roll stamp (the stamp should lightly touch the pan beneath the roll). Let rise, uncovered, 10 minutes. While rolls are rising, preheat oven to 375 degrees. Brush rolls with egg wash and sprinkle with sesame seeds, if desired. Place rolls on middle rack of oven and bake 20 minutes, or until lightly browned on top. Remove from baking sheet and let cool on wire racks.

❦

*Note: I have seen several different versions of kaiser roll recipes, one of which calls for three egg whites. I hate recipes that leave you with extra egg yolks or half a can of something that's just going to go bad in the fridge. For my version, I put the egg yolk in the dough and use the egg white to wash the crust.*

*Barley malt syrup is what gives kaiser rolls their unique flavor and texture. It might be a bit difficult to locate if you don't have a health food store nearby. Dark corn syrup is a decent substitute, or 2 teaspoons brown sugar mixed with 1 teaspoon molasses.*

*You can make your kaiser rolls larger or smaller. Divide the dough into 16 pieces to make small breakfast treats or accompaniments to salad, or into 8 pieces to make extra-large sandwich rolls.*

Bread Machine

# KAISER ROLLS

Yield: 6 rolls.

1/2 cup **water**

1/2 cup **milk**

1 **egg yolk**

1 1/2 teaspoons **dark corn syrup**

1 1/2 teaspoons **vegetable oil**

1 1/2 teaspoons **salt**

3 cups **bread flour**

1 1/2 teaspoons **FLEISCHMANN'S Bread Machine Yeast**

**Cornmeal**, for sprinkling on pan

1 **egg white** beaten with 1 tablespoon **water**, for egg wash

Add water, milk, egg yolk, corn syrup, oil, salt, bread flour and yeast to bread machine pan in the order suggested by manufacturer. Select **dough/manual cycle**.

When cycle is complete, remove dough from machine. Divide dough into 6 equal pieces. Roll each piece into a ball; flatten ball to 4-inch circle. Grease a baking sheet and sprinkle with cornmeal. Place dough circles on prepared baking sheet. Cover and let rise in a warm, draft-free place 20 minutes.

Press each roll firmly with kaiser roll stamp. Let rise, uncovered, 10 minutes. Brush with egg wash. Bake in a preheated 375-degree oven 20 minutes, or until done. Remove from baking sheet and let cool on wire rack.

# HUNGARIAN POTATO BREAD

Yield: 2 large loaves.

### SPONGE:

1 cup lukewarm **water**

2 packages **FLEISCHMANN'S Active Dry Yeast**

1 teaspoon **honey**

1 cup **bread flour**

### DOUGH:

1 cup lukewarm **water** (use potato water, if available; see note)

2 tablespoons **honey**

1 to 1 1/2 cups **mashed potatoes** (see note)

1 1/2 teaspoons **salt**

1 tablespoon **anise, fennel** or **caraway seeds** (optional)

6 to 8 cups **bread flour**

**Milk** and additional **anise, fennel** or **caraway seeds**, for topping (optional)

**For sponge:** Combine water, yeast, honey and bread flour in large bowl; beat until smooth. Let stand 20 minutes, or until foamy and doubled in volume.

**For dough:** Add water, honey, mashed potatoes, salt and anise seeds to sponge; beat until smooth. Add 2 cups of the bread flour; beat until flour is thoroughly incorporated. Repeat with 2 cups flour. Add enough of the remaining flour, about 1 cup at a time, to form a soft dough. The amount of flour will vary according to the amount of mashed potatoes you use.

Turn out dough onto lightly floured surface. Knead 8 to 10 minutes. Rinse and dry the bowl, then oil surface of dough and place dough in bowl. Cover with a clean, dry cloth and let rise in a warm, draft-free place about 1 hour, or until doubled.

Punch down dough. Knead briefly to expel large air bubbles. Divide dough into 2 equal pieces. Form each piece into a loaf. Place loaves in lightly greased 9x5x3-inch loaf pans. Cover with a clean, dry cloth and let rise about 30 minutes, or until doubled.

About 15 minutes before end of rising time, preheat oven to 375

## Bread Break

I hate seeing food go to waste, so a lot of my baking is inspired by leftovers. If creamed corn appears at supper, I'll probably make cornmeal muffins for breakfast. Leftover ham or bacon gets chopped up for pizza topping. This Hungarian Potato Bread uses leftover mashed potatoes. The size of the loaves will be determined in part by the amount of mashed potatoes you have on hand. The recipe as it stands will make two large 2-pound loaves. If you end up with a smaller amount of dough, use smaller pans. The truly traditional method would be to bake them free-form on baking stones or a lightly greased baking sheet.

degrees. If desired, brush tops of loaves with milk and sprinkle with additional anise seeds. Bake loaves 40 to 45 minutes, or until loaves are golden brown, slide easily from pan and sound hollow when tapped on bottom. Let cool on wire racks.

~

*Note: I developed this recipe on the assumption that the mashed potatoes would contain a certain amount of salt and butter or margarine. If you never have leftover mashed potatoes, you will need to cook some potatoes especially for use in this recipe. Peel and dice 2 medium potatoes. Place potatoes in a small saucepan and add enough water to cover potatoes. Boil until soft, then drain, reserving the water to use in the recipe. Mash the cooked potatoes. You'll want to increase the salt to 2 teaspoons and add 2 tablespoons butter along with the mashed potatoes.*

*Although using fennel or caraway seeds is traditional, I prefer this bread without any seasoning. Then you can really taste the difference the potatoes make.*

# HUNGARIAN POTATO BREAD

Yield: 1 (1 ¹/₂-pound) loaf.

1 cup **potato water** (reserved from boiling potatoes)

3 tablespoons **milk**

2 tablespoons **honey**

1 tablespoon **butter** or **margarine**

¹/₂ cup boiled and **mashed potato**

1 ¹/₄ teaspoons **salt**

3 cups **bread flour**

1 ¹/₂ teaspoons **FLEISCHMANN'S Bread Machine Yeast**

Add potato water, milk, honey, butter, mashed potato, salt, bread flour and yeast to bread machine pan in the order suggested by manufacturer. Select **basic cycle; medium/normal color setting**.

~

# SALLY LUNN

Yield: 2 loaves.

1 package **FLEISCHMANN'S Active Dry Yeast**

$^1/_2$ cup lukewarm **water**

1 $^1/_2$ cups **cream**, warmed

3 **eggs**, at room temperature, lightly beaten

$^1/_4$ cup **granulated sugar**

1 teaspoon **salt**

Dash **ground nutmeg**

4 cups **all-purpose flour**

Sprinkle yeast over lukewarm water in large bowl; stir until dissolved. Add cream, eggs, sugar, salt and nutmeg; stir well. Stir in flour, 1 cup at a time, beating after each addition until well mixed. Batter will be thick. Cover bowl and let rise in a warm, draft-free place about 1 hour, or until doubled.

You will need two empty 46-ounce juice cans. Remove labels and wash cans. Lightly grease cans. Cut a circle of waxed paper or parchment paper to fit in the bottom of each can; place in cans. Divide batter between the two prepared cans. The batter should fill cans about one-third full. Cover and let rise 45 to 60 minutes, or until doubled.

About 15 minutes before end of rising time, preheat oven to 375 degrees. Place cans on a baking sheet. Bake 35 to 40 minutes, or until cake tester inserted in center comes out clean and bread is pulling away from sides of can. If the tops seem to be browning too quickly, lightly cover tops with aluminum foil about halfway through baking time. Place cans on wire rack to cool at least 45 minutes before removing bread from cans. Let bread cool completely on wire rack.

※

*Note: If you don't use juice in large cans, ask the staff at the local school cafeteria to save a couple for you. Soak off the labels. Be sure to remove as much of the glue as possible because it will melt in the oven and can make a mess. As I was developing my version of this recipe, I tried pouring all the batter into one can and only letting it rise a little before baking. The batter erupted out of the can like lava from a volcano, spilled all over the oven and fused the can to the oven rack!*

## Bread Break

There are two possible origins for the name of this light golden tea cake. The one usually given in England is that they are named after a 17th-century pastry cook named Sally Lunn who was a Huguenot fleeing the persecutions under Louis XIV. She settled in Bath, England, and opened a shop that specialized in light tea cakes. The building that housed her bakery was renovated in the 1930s, and the original ovens were uncovered in the basement. The original recipe is a closely guarded secret passed on with the deed of the building.

The other explanation given for this unusual name is that it is a corruption of the French *soleil et lune* (sun and moon). The bread is a golden color, and is often served sliced horizontally with butter, clotted cream or whipped cream spread on the layers.

# FROM MY KITCHEN ANGEL

# Barbecued Beef Brisket

Yield: 8 to 10 servings.

Bread Break

My friend Matt, who is the head honcho in marketing at KETC/Channel 9 in St. Louis, travels with me when I go on media tours and appearances. While we were in an airport some-where, we were brain-storming about recipes, and he suggested something to go with barbecued beef brisket, something hearty and Texas-sized. The result was Texas Moppin' Rolls (page 36). But it hardly seems fair to make rolls to accompany barbecue with-out providing a recipe for the beef! My kitchen angel Bridget once again came through with a real winner. The camera crew were happy to sample this after the episode was taped. I have no doubt that real Texans will take issue with any number of the details here, so we offer the recipe as the modest attempt of barbecue amateurs!

1 **beef brisket** (about 8 pounds)

### Dry Rub:

1 tablespoon **chili powder**

1 tablespoon **ground cumin**

2 tablespoons **salt**

2 tablespoons **cracked black pepper**

3 tablespoons minced **garlic**

$1/2$ cup packed **dark brown sugar**

### Barbecue Sauce:

2 tablespoons **olive oil**

1 cup chopped **green bell pepper**

1 cup chopped **red onion**

$1/8$ teaspoon **cayenne pepper**

$1/4$ teaspoon **ground coriander**

$1/4$ teaspoon **ground ginger**

$1/4$ teaspoon **crushed red pepper**

$1/2$ teaspoon **dry mustard**

3 tablespoons minced **garlic**

1 tablespoon **ground black pepper**

Juice of 1 **lemon** (about 3 tablespoons)

$1/2$ cup **tomato paste**

$1/4$ cup **red wine vinegar**

1 cup **ketchup**

$1/4$ cup **Dijon-style mustard**

1 cup packed **brown sugar**

1 (14.5-ounce) can **stewed tomatoes**, undrained

$1/4$ cup **water**

Using a sharp knife, score the brisket by making $1/2$-inch-deep cuts into the flesh every 2 to 3 inches, cutting across the grain of the meat on both sides, forming a crisscross pattern on both sides, which allows the flavors to penetrate and tenderize the meat.

Prepare dry rub by mixing chili powder, cumin, salt, pepper, garlic and brown sugar in a small bowl. Pat dry rub mixture all over brisket. Place brisket in roasting pan. Brisket can be roasted imme-diately or refrigerated up to 24 hours.

Roast in a preheated 350-degree oven 3 to 4 hours, depending on size of brisket (allow about 30 minutes per pound). Brisket is done when fork tender. The flesh will feel very soft when pressed with your finger. Cover the brisket with foil after 1 or 1 1/2 hours, because the sugar in the rub will burn. (Do not dismay if it does burn; the brisket will still be fine and tasty.) Let brisket stand 10 minutes after removing from oven, then slice thin on an angled 45-degree bias across the grain for maximum tenderness.

While brisket is roasting, prepare barbecue sauce. Heat oil in large skillet. Add green pepper and onion; cook and stir until translucent. Add cayenne, coriander, ginger, hot red pepper flakes, dry mustard, garlic and pepper; cook and stir 1 minute. Add lemon juice, tomato paste, vinegar, ketchup, mustard, brown sugar, stewed tomatoes with their liquid, and water. Simmer, stirring occasionally, about 30 minutes, or until sauce thickens and flavors blend. Sauce will be slightly spicy, thick and rich in flavor.

Serve sliced brisket with barbecue sauce.

# CHICKEN SOUP

Yield: 3 quarts.

3 tablespoons **olive oil**

1/2 cup diced **carrots**

1/2 cup diced **celery**

1 cup peeled **pearl onions** (small and sweet; can substitute 1 cup chopped onion)

1 tablespoon minced **garlic** (or 1 teaspoon garlic powder or granulated garlic)

1 **bay leaf**

1/2 teaspoon **dried thyme**

1 large bunch **fresh parsley**, coarsely chopped (or 1 tablespoon dried parsley flakes)

4 (15-ounce) cans **chicken broth**

2 cups chopped **cooked chicken**

*Bread Break*

One can never have too many soup recipes. This one is excellent with Sage Dumplings (page 94). This chicken soup really is "good for what ails you," as my mother used to say. If you make your own chicken stock or broth, by all means use it. My kitchen angel Bridget makes (to use her term) "killer" chicken stock, which when refrigerated is as thick as Jell-O!

Heat oil in large skillet. Add carrots, celery and onions; cook and stir 5 minutes, or until translucent. Add garlic; cook and stir 1 minute. Add bay leaf, thyme, parsley and chicken broth; simmer 15 minutes. Add chicken; heat through. Serve hot.

# BAKED BEANS

Yield: About 3 quarts.

## Bread Break

My kitchen angel Bridget can always be relied upon to come up with a terrific recipe on the spot. When we were taping the episode *Unique Pans*, I told her it would be nice to have baked beans to accompany Boston Brown Bread (page 25). A quick consultation with a couple of cookbooks, a trip to the nearby grocery, and Bridget had this dish underway. Knowing that viewers would ask for the recipe, I asked her to keep a careful record of what she used. I especially like the use of several kinds of beans. It might be a bit unorthodox, but it makes the beans more visually appealing. Remember, we eat with our eyes first!

$^3/_4$ pound **bacon**, cut into
  $^1/_2$-inch pieces

1 cup chopped **red onion**

1 rib **celery**, chopped
  (about $^1/_2$ cup)

$^1/_2$ cup chopped **green
  bell pepper**

1 tablespoon minced **garlic**
  (3 to 4 cloves)

$^1/_4$ teaspoon **crushed red
  pepper**

1 cup **ketchup**

1 cup **barbecue sauce**

$^1/_2$ cup **maple-flavored syrup**

$^1/_4$ cup **molasses**

$^1/_2$ cup **yellow mustard**

1 teaspoon freshly **ground
  black pepper**

1 (15-ounce) can **cannellini
  beans** (or Great Northern
  beans), drained

1 (15-ounce) can **lima beans**,
  drained

1 (15-ounce) can **kidney
  beans**, drained

1 (15-ounce) can **black
  beans**, drained

1 (15-ounce) can **butter
  beans**, drained

1 teaspoon **salt**

Cook bacon in a steep-sided, heavy-bottomed saucepan until lightly crisp. Drain off most of the fat, leaving about 3 tablespoons. Add onion, celery and green pepper; cook and stir about 5 minutes, or until translucent or shiny. Add garlic, hot red pepper flakes, ketchup, barbecue sauce, maple syrup, molasses, mustard and pepper. Simmer about 30 minutes, stirring occasionally, or until sauce is slightly thickened.

Transfer bacon mixture to a bean pot or baking dish. Add cannellini, lima, kidney, black and butter beans; stir to mix. Cover and bake in a preheated 350-degree oven about 2 hours, or until beans are tender and sauce is thick and rich. Add salt, stir and serve.

# POTATO SOUP

Yield: About 4 quarts.

3 tablespoons **olive oil**

1 cup chopped **celery** (about 2 ribs)

2 cups chopped **onions**

**Ham bone** (either one large bone or 2 or 3 small bones)

1 **bay leaf**

3 tablespoons **chicken base** (or 3 chicken bouillon cubes)

2 quarts hot **tap water**

1 tablespoon minced **garlic**

12 cups (about 5 pounds) cubed **white** or **golden potatoes** ($^{1}/_{2}$-inch cubes)

2 cups chopped **cooked ham**

2 cups **sour cream**

Heat oil in a steep-sided, heavy-bottomed pot. Add celery and onions; cook and stir over medium-high heat about 5 minutes, or until vegetables are translucent. Add ham bone(s) and bay leaf. In a separate container, stir chicken base into hot water to make chicken broth. Add garlic to mixture in pot; cook no more than 1 minute. Immediately add potatoes and chicken broth; bring to a boil. Reduce heat and simmer about 20 minutes, or until potatoes are tender and fall apart when poked with a fork. Remove and discard bay leaf. Remove ham bone(s) and pull off any good ham scraps; return ham scraps to soup along with the chopped cooked ham. Discard ham bone(s). Stir in sour cream. Heat through, but do not boil. Mash or blend the soup if you like, or serve it chunky. If you blend the soup, add the ham afterward.

## Bread Break

I must confess I don't much care for potato soup, although I love many soups and stews with potatoes in them. Often when we are brainstorming about recipes and serving suggestions, potato soup comes up as a perennial favorite of station personnel, so we included it in one of our episodes.

Every time I serve a soup on camera, we get requests for the recipe, even if I never actually demonstrate how to make the soup at any point in the program! I've learned to make sure we keep track of Bridget's off-camera creations.

# Pear-Apple Chutney

Yield: About 2 cups.

*Bread Break*

Here's another accompaniment to bread from my kitchen angel Bridget. I asked her to develop a sweet chutney with a relatively mild flavor to use as a topping for a turkey sandwich made with Onion Rolls (page 88). She gave me two from which to choose: one that was much spicier, and this sweet and subtle blend of pears and apples. It's so good it could stand as a side dish on its own and would be excellent on top of Overnight Multigrain Waffles (page 18) or as one of the layers between slices of Sally Lunn (page 115).

$^1/_2$ cup **dried cranberries**

3 **d'Anjou pears**, peeled and cut into $^1/_4$- to $^1/_2$-inch cubes

1 firm, **sweet-tart apple** (such as Braeburn or Granny Smith), peeled and cut into $^1/_4$- to $^1/_2$-inch cubes

1 (4-inch) piece **root fennel**, finely chopped (optional)

1 rib **celery**, finely chopped

$^1/_4$ teaspoon **cayenne pepper**

$^1/_2$ teaspoon **dry mustard**

$^1/_4$ cup **orange juice**

2 tablespoons **honey**

$^1/_4$ cup **rice vinegar** (or any mild vinegar such as champagne, white wine or distilled white)

$^1/_4$ cup **granulated sugar**

Combine cranberries, pears, apple, fennel, celery, cayenne, dry mustard, orange juice, honey, rice vinegar and sugar in a nonreactive saucepan (not aluminum or cast iron); stir to mix well. Simmer, stirring frequently, 30 to 45 minutes, or until liquid is reduced and mixture thickens. Let cool, then ladle into clean containers with tight-fitting lids. Refrigerate for up to two weeks.

# General Index

# Bread Machine Recipes

# TV Series Episodes

# About St. Bede Abbey

St. Bede Abbey is a Benedictine monastery set among farms and wooded bluffs overlooking the Illinois River in Peru, Illinois. The community was established in 1890.

Daily life for the 35 monks who live there includes time spent in morning, noon and evening prayer; daily Mass; private prayer; and spiritual reading. The men also teach at St. Bede Academy, a college preparatory school; minister to area parishes; and work at maintaining the monastery's buildings, grounds and enterprises.

The abbey's orchard has over 1,200 apple trees and is open for business from mid-August to early November. Honey from the abbey apiary is in demand throughout the Illinois Valley. A busy print shop is also on the monastery premises. Within the monastic community, members perform a variety of services reflecting their diverse interests and abilities: business manager, candle maker, barber, plumber, electrician, gardener, organist, sculptor, writer, singer and auto mechanic.

Men and women who wish to visit the monastery or spend time on retreat are welcome to contact the abbey directly. More information about St. Bede is available at *http://www.theramp. net/stbede.* To support the abbey's mission, write to: Office of Mission Advancement, St. Bede Abbey, Peru, IL 61354.

TERRI GATES